WAIT

WAIT

KATHY WILLIAMS

DEEDS PUBLISHING | ATHENS, GA

Copyright © 2024 — Kathy Williams

ALL RIGHTS RESERVED—No part of this book may be reproduced in any form or by any electronic or mechanical means, including information storage and retrieval systems, without permission in writing from the authors, except by a reviewer who may quote brief passages in a review.

Published by Deeds Publishing in Athens, GA
www.deedspublishing.com

Printed in The United States of America

Cover and interior design by Deeds Publishing

ISBN 978-1-961505-37-7

Books are available in quantity for promotional or premium use. For information, email info@deedspublishing.com.

First Edition, 2025

10 9 8 7 6 5 4 3 2 1

"Beware the deadly donkey falling slowly from the sky. You may choose the way you live but not the way you die."

—Hallmark birthday card

For Doug, beloved and missed.

D.O.E.

Tales from the Third Shift and Other Stories

This book is dedicated to all who work the Third Shift.

Introduction

I spent nearly 22 years in the Convenience Store Industry. I was at a crossroads in my life and my mother suggested that I get a job at The Food Flash. It was really Flash Foods, but I knew what she meant. It seems the manager there was very kind to my mother, and she wanted to return the favor by convincing me to work there. I intended to stay two months. Flash Foods gave me one opportunity after another. They recognized hard work and loyalty, and I will always appreciate what they gave me in return. Best company ever!

    I will always be grateful for the people I met who enriched my life and taught me so many valuable life lessons. The most important one being that people are more than a D.O.E., Direct Operating Expense.

From Third Shift to Store Manager

My first shift working alone was on a Friday night, 11 p.m.–7 a.m. I trained with the store manager during the day on Tuesday, Wednesday, and Thursday. Now it was time to face my first shift by myself. Working alone was intimidating enough. Adding to my stress was the fact that I would be working during the night. The scary time.

I clocked in on the time sheet then changed the VCR tape and logged it. If anyone was going to come into the store to rob and kill me, I was going to make sure there was a recording of it. At this time each tape ran for eight hours, the same timeframe as our shifts. Each person was responsible for the recording of their shift.

The store was busy with workers from the area restaurants and those out for a good time. Business was steady. I was inexperienced and slow on the cash register but competent enough, so the checkout line did not get too long. So far, so good. Everyone was in a good mood. Then it happened. The worst thing ever. The register tape ran out. You need to understand that it was a huge taboo to let the register tape run out. It was forbidden to ring up anyone unless you had the register tape going. I really did not know the reason at that time, but later learned that all of our sales records were derived from the register tape. All the gas sales, all of the voids, all of the taxes, the everything of Flash Foods depended upon the register tape. It was the God of Flash Foods.

My head began to sweat. I sweated to the point that there were drops running down the side of my face. I popped open the side of the register and looked at the diagram. We had not changed the register tape during my training. Surely I could figure out this engineering nightmare! I stuck the tape here. I pushed it there. I tugged and sweated while the checkout line got longer and longer. The faces of the customers got darker and darker. Muttering was going on. There were deep sighs. There was the rolling of eyes. I sweated so much the back of my blouse was wet. Surely, I would soon begin to stink a sour stench of panic and fear.

Then the sweetest sound permeated my sweat-filled ears, "Honey, would you let me help you? I think this is the same kind of register that I use at my work."

I looked up to a vision of angelic loveliness in the face of the most wonderful human being in the world. I immediately flouted company policy and brought her behind the checkout. In a flash she taught me the ebb and flow of cash register tape engineering. I never forgot this lesson. Never, never, never.

I thanked her and would have promised her my firstborn but as my firstborn was almost of college age, I figured she might prefer a newborn, so I kept that thought to myself.

Never underestimate how powerful a simple act of kindness can be.

Company policy. No one is allowed behind the checkout except company employees who are on the clock.

Company policy. No one is allowed to perform any work at Flash Foods unless they are a company employee who is on the clock.

First night on the job I freely, willing, desperately violated two company policies! Maybe no one will watch my tape of that night! Ha!!

* * *

His name was Felix, or at least that is what he told me. He was a very elderly gentleman who would come into the store every day and buy one bottle of O'Doul's, a non-alcoholic beer.

As a new clerk, I was very strict about adhering to our policy of checking the IDs on all tobacco and alcohol purchases. O'Doul's was considered one of those purchases. This first encounter with Felix demanded that I ask for his ID, even though it was obvious that he was of age. Some customers would get mad when I asked for their IDs, telling me how stupid I was not to be omnipotent and know their age. Others were delighted that I asked, erroneously believing that I thought they were younger than they looked. This was not the case. I carded everyone. I could not afford to lose my job (I had three hungry children and instead of a crop in the field, I had a husband) nor could I chance getting caught in a sting operation and be charged with selling to a minor.

Anyhow, Felix brought his O'Doul's to the checkout counter. I smilingly asked for his ID. He lit up, grinning from ear to ear. He whipped out a worn, faded brown wallet. Down on the counter he plunked a photo ID.

This ID was most unusual to say the least. On it was the photograph of a man with an enormous erect penis. This penis was probably two feet long, maybe more. I was not to be outdone, however. I said, "Felix, this is not a Flash Foods approved ID. We only accept a valid driver's license, a state ID card, a passport, or a government ID. I am afraid that as remarkable as this one is, I cannot accept it." It was all I could do to retain a professional manner and inside I was laughing hysterically.

Well, Felix finally produced a valid ID, but I **NEVER** asked him for his ID again, even though every day when he entered the store he said, "Do you want to see my ID?" HA!!!!

* * *

When I worked midnights, I got to meet some "unusual" people. People of the night are interesting, scary, amusing, but above all else, most entertaining. One of these was a homeless man I referred to as "Numbers Man."

He was probably in his late thirties, white, stocky with dark hair and a beard that was closely shaved. He was always attired in blue jean cut-off shorts and wore a T-shirt. He had very well-developed calves. I assumed this was from his constant wanderings. He walked all over Valdosta and would visit as many convenience stores as he could every night. We would often call other stores and let them know of any goings ons, unusual, dangerous, or just entertaining. We all got to know "Numbers Man" very well.

The first night he came in he introduced himself to me and told me how he liked to wander. He then asked to see my right palm. He then declared that I had the number three. He went on to inform me of how this number was unique to me and how it related to Jesus. He was quite a storyteller. After a while he stated he needed to move on after he got a cup of coffee. He had his own cup. This saved him money since he only had to pay a refill price. He was at the coffee counter preparing his coffee while I waited on other customers.

After he left, another customer came in for coffee and complained there were no condiments available for his coffee. It seems "Numbers Man" had absconded with all of the sugar, Sweet' N Low, and creamer. Hmm, I thought, he won't get away with this again.

Two nights later he returned. I told him he could not wipe me out of condiments, and he could only use what he needed for his current cup of coffee. He then asked if I would give him a couple of dollars if he picked up the cigarette butts in the parking lot. I relented. After all he was homeless, even if it was by his choice and I also knew he had some conning skills. When he finished in the parking lot, I paid him two dollars out of my own pocket. He then asked me if he could have a couple of straws. I said, "Ok, but nothing else."

To my great astonishment he proceeded to join the two straws together and place a cigarette butt at the very end. He then lit the cigarette butt and left, happily smoking, and blowing rings!

* * *

Around 2 a.m. a giggly, intoxicated couple entered the store, kissing, groping, and veering from one side of the snack isle to the other. They were having a large time. They asked me the way to the bathroom. I pointed them in the right direction to the back of the store and continued to wait upon customers.

I had a fair number of customers to ring up and everyone seemed to be in a blissful state of joy and silliness; most had obviously been indulging in adult beverages. It was a nice crowd who were determined to make the most of their altered states.

As the store cleared out I noticed that the couple who had gone to the bathroom were still there. Hmm. More customers entered the store.

After about 20 minutes, they staggered to the front door. They were even more disheveled than when they had arrived earlier. Hmm. Maybe I had better check the bathroom. Surely they did not…

Yes, they had. To the point of removing the bathroom sink from its foundation. Well. Now how am I supposed to report this one?

I got out the maintenance log. This was an official Flash form. Let's see. The store number is first. Ok, no problem. The date is next. Ok, no problem. The description is next. Ok, bathroom sink is no longer on its foundation. How did this occur was next. Well. Hmm. Suspect sexual activity of a vigorous nature? Hmm. Suspect minor earthquake in South Georgia? Hmm. Sudden violent rodent activity inside the walls causing separation from foundation? Hmm.

I decided to leave this to the "Great Unknown".

In bold letters I put **"Only God knows."**

***

When I reported to work one midnight, I had a note from the store manager for me to clean the Jet Spray machine. Beside the note was a laminated instruction sheet on how to drain, take apart, clean, and put the machine back together. Hmm.

The Jet Spray machine had two tanks, each with a different, colorful flavor of a sugary Kool-Aid-like beverage. Inside each tank an attractive fountain regurgitated these flavors in a never-ending spray that dazzled small children into begging their parents to buy one for them. It was absolute junk.

Around 2 a.m., the store was finally empty of customers, and I proceeded to my Jet Spray chore. Draining the product went well, even though I got enough on me to draw flies should any enter the store. I was pretty sticky.

I removed all parts and washed them in the backroom sink. I had to stop and wait on some customers who remarked about my colorful Jet Spray shirt. Seems I even had some in my hair.

I returned to the machine and endeavored to put all the parts back. To my horror, there were two pieces left over. I read the instruction sheet once again. Maybe these pieces were not that necessary. Hmm.

I had some more customers. I went back to the machine. It was now close to 4 a.m. and I would soon start to get very busy with the early morning crowd, so I needed to wrap this spray thing up.

I went ahead and did a trial run with only water in the tanks to see how things would go. They went badly. Water leaked all over the counter and onto the floor. Just then a group of early morning hunters came in and gave me grief over the mess and took up twenty minutes of my time.

I returned to the machine and took it apart again. Customers kept coming in. The next thing I knew it was time for my manager to arrive. I still did not have the machine back together.

When she arrived, I was busy with customers. She saw my incomplete Jet Spray mess. She quickly took over running the cash register and let me go back to my evil Jet Spray. I had figured out that the two pieces were seals to prevent leakage and I finally managed to get them in the right place.

Perhaps I will earn a degree in convenience store equipment engineering if this keeps up.

**

There is nothing like going to work in a convenience store full of goods that include alcohol and tobacco to bring out the true character of "friends" and family. It will also test your ability to resist corruption. I experienced this firsthand.

One night when I was still working midnights, my brother-in-law and a jockey that worked for him (who had in the past worked for me) came into the store around 10 p.m. They hung around until all the customers had left. Obviously they wanted to speak to me alone.

"Say, how about letting us have a 12 pack of Bud."

"Are you crazy? That is dishonest! That is stealing! I could lose my job and go to jail!"

"No, you won't. We won't tell anyone."

"You don't have to tell anyone. I will not steal and besides we are being recorded as we speak."

"No one has time to watch all those videos. We will stay out of camera range anyhow."

"You have to walk out the door and it is on camera 24-7."

"You mean you won't help us out?"

"No. Get out!"

They hung around for nearly an hour. I finally told them that I was going to call both my husband and the police if they did not leave.

This firsthand experience did give me valuable insight on how hard it is to resist your "friends" and family when they pressure you for favors. I could relate more easily to employee theft when I later had to investigate and prosecute for it. It also showed me the true relationship that I had with members of my own family as well as "friends."

* * *

It was the first time I had done the bank deposit alone. My store was a low-volume store and except for two shifts during the week, we were always single-shifted. This meant that we surreptitiously worked the deposit under the counter between customers, hoping no one noticed the neatly stacked bills.

This happened to be a bright, sunny Saturday and I had completed all the necessary paperwork by 10:30 a.m., lacking only the finalization of the deposit. I was nervously anticipating the end of the task, looking forward to securing the money in the safe where it would be unavailable until I was relieved and headed to the bank.

A lone customer came into the store and handed me his money for his purchase. His hands were shaking uncontrollably as I reached for it. Suddenly every hair on my head stood up and sweat poured from my skull. I began to tremble, and I became nauseous. Surely he was about to rob me!! Why else would he be shaking so profoundly?!

Just before I let out an involuntary shriek, I suddenly noticed that his coveralls were unzipped with a flaccid penis hanging languidly, displayed for the entire world to see. What in the world?? A pervert, just what I needed on my first venture into the world of "Convenience Store Banking!!!"

I was so relieved that I was not being robbed that all I could say was, "Thank you sir, have a nice day."

What I wish I had said was, "Thank you sir. I hope you and your flaccid penis have a nice day!"

* * *

I was pulling another double, which meant that I was working from seven in the morning until eleven that night. I was pretty bummed out about it because it meant once again I was not home to help with homework or make dinner for my three children. I was lucky that my oldest daughter was very capable of filling in for me, but I always hated for her to have to be the temporary "Mom." I tried to look on the bright side, knowing the extra shift would bring in much needed income.

The night dragged on. While I was hungry, I could not afford the expense of buying a meal from the store or any of the surrounding fast food joints. I would just have to wait until I got home.

Around 8:30 p.m., one of my regulars came in. She lived within a few yards of the store, and I always enjoyed seeing her. Lately she had been pretty stressed due to her husband's illness. His illness was very serious, something he might not be able to recover from. One thing that convenience store people learn to do is to listen to our customers' problems, joys, trials, and tribulations. We are like the bartender in the bar, a ready sounding board of compassion and understanding. Sometimes their stories were very entertaining!

She was surprised to see me since once I had become manager, I usually only worked first shift. I explained that my second shift had a sick child she needed to stay home with, so I was pulling the shift in her place. She asked me if I had been able to go home in between the two shifts and I said no. "Well, that means you haven't had a thing to eat, have you?" She knew that I always packed my lunch, so she assumed I was doing without my dinner. "I will be right back!" and out the door she went with a smile on her face.

She returned about 30 minutes later with a plate steaming with home cooked mustard greens, scratch-made corn muffins, and bacon that had come from their own butchered pig! She even brought some hot sauce to season with!

As I ate we visited. I listened as she detailed the latest treatments she was taking her husband to. For her to show me such generosity and kindness in the midst of the terrible time she and her husband were going through touched me profoundly. I can still smell the greens, savor the moist tender muffins, and taste the crunch of the bacon. But most of all I can remember the relationship we shared and that moment of kindness.

* * *

He was known as the "Newport Napper" because he only stole Newport cigarettes. He made his "Napper" runs during the middle of the night. He rode a bicycle with a basket on the front of it. He would come into a store and go directly to wherever the Newports were, grab as many cartons as he could carry, and rush back out the door, leap on his bike, and take off. He never showed any weapons, but it was still disconcerting to have him pay you a visit.

I got the call from my assistant manager around one in the morning. She was hysterical. The "Newport Napper" had struck our store for the first time. She was very young, and her husband was in the Air Force. We were short-staffed and she and I had been alternating the midnight shift. I calmed her down and told her I was on the way. I called my supervisor to let him know.

When I arrived, I played the VCR tape for the police. We completed all the necessary paperwork and I prepared to go back home. My assistant had calmed down and told me she was fine and could continue the shift by herself.

I started driving home and noticed a vehicle behind me. It was a small pickup with a man driving. There was very little traffic out. As we headed out of town he was still behind me. Once we got to a deserted part of the highway he all of a sudden pulled up beside me. He was making an obscene motion indicating masturbation. He was trying to get me to pull over. I sped up with him still beside me. The highway was a two-lane road, so he was driving on the wrong side. We reached speeds up to ninety miles an hour. I was thinking, "Ok, Kathy dummy, where do you think you are going? You cannot go home because you have to stop and open a gate." So I was trying to think of a way to head to either an open store or the nearest police station. After about six miles of this, he all of a sudden fell back and disappeared. I watched for some time and then finally reached my turnoff and arrived safely home. I called the incident in, but I never heard anything about a resolution to the incident.

Life in the Flash Lane has more than one hazard to overcome. Give me a "Newport Napper" any day over some weirdo pervert.

* * *

I was awakened by a phone call in the early morning. The midnight girl on the other end was babbling on about a robbery and it was a few minutes before I figured out that it was not my store but one of our other ones. This girl was a pretty new employee who had started less than two weeks before and I already knew she was not going to last long. First of all she was not a great worker. She believed her job meant holding up the checkout counter.

By the time I got to the store and relieved her, the store phone was ringing off the hook. Other store managers let me know that one of our stores had been robbed, but even worse, the employee on duty had been shot and killed. Information and rumor were running rampant as to who this employee was. It could have been anyone, because managers or store personnel from other stores may have been pulling that shift since we helped each other out as needed.

Later we learned that Jane, who had been training for a management position, had been found shot to death by some Walmart employees getting off work around midnight. It seems that Jane had been on a step ladder filling the fountain machine with ice when she was shot. Tragically there was no video of the shooting. Evidently Jane had failed to change the VCR tape when she came on duty, something each shift at that time was required to do.

I do not remember when my supervisor came and talked to me about the killing. I do remember he was distraught, telling me that he had to clean her brains from the floor and ceiling. Jane was a single mom with two children. The majority of convenience store employees are single moms. Most of the men in their lives are deadbeats that rarely pay child support and these women are burdened with the task of raising their children with minimum wage, low prestige jobs that demand they work long hours to make ends meet. As you can imagine, if a single mom pulls extra shifts to get overtime pay, the children are often left with relatives or alone since the cost of childcare is unaffordable. Only well-off women can indulge in the luxuries of childcare. Also, it is almost unheard of to find a childcare provider for second and third shift workers. I constantly struggled to help my working mothers find ways to work while not leaving their children in unsupervised situations. More than once I had moms whose teenage children started to have problems because their mothers had to work second and third shifts. These kids were old enough to be left alone, but then ended up with the wrong crowd and running the streets at night.

Jane's murder terrified the convenience store workers in Valdosta. No one would work third shift and third shift people quit in droves. I ended up working from 11 p.m. until 4 p.m. the next day for nearly six months. Was I terrified? You bet I was. I had no recourse. I needed my job to feed my children, pay the bills, and keep my head above water. Every day customers would come into the store and tell me that I was crazy to work for these people. "They don't care anything about you," was the standard conversation. That did not help my anxiety.

Rumors were so numerous that it just about made you sick. One fact that came out concerned a robbery our company had at another store just two weeks prior to Jane's killing. Two masked black men had shot their way into the store and robbed it but did not kill the cashier. This store was in a bad neighborhood and had a night window that was operated during late second shift and all of third shift. The robbers just shot the door out and came in anyway. I knew the cashier who had been on duty, and it was she who first told me that the cops determined through ballistics that the same gun that killed Jane was the one used to rob her. There was video of that robbery, but they wore masks, making identification difficult.

Every night the killing was on the news. This did not help me one bit as I tried to sleep for four hours before I would head to the store for seventeen or more hours. I did not get a day off in those six months. One night I was so tired that I fell asleep standing up and tumbled against the cigarette rack. It was a really horrible time. I tried not to think about what would happen to my children should I get killed. I concentrated on trying to appreciate the fact that I was making extra money for pulling all these shifts no one else would work.

It would be nearly a year before an arrest was made in Jane's killing. A thug who called himself "Baby Doc Holiday" ended up being sent to jail. His picture in the paper showed him smirking and smiling as he appeared to enjoy his notoriety and fame. How ironic that he fashioned himself after Doc Holiday, who had lived in Valdosta prior to his gun fighting days out west.

The company installed a night window in my store and that did give some comfort, even though in the back of my mind I could not help but remember that it did not stop robbers from shooting your door open and robbing you anyway.

* * *

After the death of Jane, the hysteria in Valdosta was palpable. Any business that operated during the midnight hours struggled to keep those hours staffed. One of the strategies that the police employed was to post "shoot to kill police" in the backrooms of convenience stores.

My store was well suited for this. The backroom had a small one-way view window from which the officer could easily monitor all activity inside the store. I was instructed not to allow anyone into the backroom the nights that the officer was there. The public bathroom was in the backroom, and I was to post a sign stating that it was out of order. I never knew ahead of time when the officer would be in my store.

I was told that should a robber come in and rob me, I was to drop to the ground. Wonderful. Just drop to the ground while they shoot the robber and hope their aim is good. This was not a great time to be at work. It was extremely unnerving. I felt like bait, yet at the same time, I wanted them to catch the killer.

***

I was pulling another midnight. True to form, my "sorry" third shift person called out at the last minute on a Friday night. She had done this the weekend before, only it was on Saturday.

She said something about, "My Aunt Liddie died, and I need to be there for my mother." The problem was I was pretty certain that she had buried "Aunt Liddie" about two months prior, another time she unexpectedly had to take a weekend night off. My boss sarcastically said all I could do was deal with it, "Do you think midnight people grow on trees? Am I supposed to give birth to these people?" I fumed as I thought about all the dead that seemed to only die or be buried on weekends. As a store manager it was my wonderful responsibility to cover the shift.

Around 2:30 in the morning, a customer pulled up to the store and rang the bell on the night window. The night window was new, having been installed less than a month before. These windows are an anathema to corporate as they symbolize unsafe surroundings and cause a drop in sales.

This customer was unique. He had a very dark shadow of a beard, was dressed in a black and white-striped mini dress with a wide red belt. He sported red high heels, accessorized with a fetching red purse. Haphazardly perched upon his head was an ill-fitting black wig that framed his very masculine features in such an endearing way that I immediately liked him, even if he was on the weird side. It sure beat the hell out of a guy in a mask carrying a gun.

I opened the night window. He asked for a pack of Marlboro Reds in a box. As he spoke he gave me a big smile. I got his cigarettes and watched as he turned to leave. He gave me a big "shit eating grin" as he turned away, dress tucked up under his belt, rotating a big, white, shiny, but extremely hairy behind. Brouhaha!! Nothing like some "Ass in a Flash" I thought to myself. Maybe I would send a suggestion to corporate to use "Ass in a Flash" for upcoming marketing promotions!

* * *

I found her in the backroom when I went to organize it. She was half of a manikin. The top half. What in the world was a half manikin doing in the backroom of a convenience store? Hmm. I later found out that she had been a manikin refugee from Belk's when she no longer had all functioning parts. The area supervisor's wife at the time worked for Belk's and he brought the manikin to this store for employees to use in merchandising displays. We often decorated for the seasons as well as for various product promotions. I named her Flash Food Frannie.

When you work the midnight shift it can be lonely. When I worked in the backroom I found myself talking to Frannie. Hmm. "Must be losing it," I thought.

Once I became the store manager, I continually found ways to use her for promotions. The one that I enjoyed the most was dressing her up as a Vampire and putting her in the Bud Light Castle display that the Bud guy built in the center of the store for Halloween. She was a big hit with the customers. She was realistic enough to actually cause some customers to momentarily be startled and somewhat frightened. I even had some small children screech when they saw her.

One morning during this time I came into the store and saw that Frannie had a black garbage bag over her head and torso. My midnight man was finishing up in the cooler as he prepared to leave. As he came out of the cooler he pointed his finger at Frannie, "I cannot work with that demon woman, and

I won't work with that demon woman. Either she goes or I go!" I stood there with my mouth wide open as he clocked out and stormed out the door.

It seemed that every time he came around the corner from the backroom she was staring at him with "her vampire teeth and glowing eyes."

I did not want to lose him as an employee, so we compromised to cover her during the midnight shift and reveal her during the day. While this is the complete opposite of vampire behavior, we found that it was the best for him, even though he had to endure a lot of ribbing from his nightly customers!

* * *

It was New Year's Eve, and I was working the midnight shift. I was the manager but once again some employee had suffered a "cataclysmic" event and could not come in so here I was.

It was a very busy night. Everyone was happy except me. I kept reminding myself that I would enjoy the extra money, but so far this had not translated into any joy.

Then a group of university students came in. All were guys and seemed to float around the store as they grabbed up every bag of chips and dip in the store. "Hmm. Must have the munchies," I thought to myself.

As I rang them up they asked about me having to pull the midnight. It seems they knew that I normally no longer worked this shift and they commiserated with me on my misfortune. This prompted one of them to confer with the rest and they then proceeded to entertain me, as well as the other customers in the store. They were members of the university glee club.

They arranged themselves in a chorus line and began to dance and sing "*My Girl*"! This was followed by four or five more songs accompanied with a dance routine. Customers in the store joined in the singing and we had quite the party!

Without a doubt this still remains my most memorable New Year's Eve. And all because I was forced to pull a most unwelcome shift!

Supervision

We had some stores with car washes. Therefore, we had car wash stories. One of my favorite ones was told to me by the supervisor who was in charge of my training as I moved from store manager to field training supervisor.

There are height restrictions for entering a car wash as well as rules regarding stuff in the backs of pickup trucks. You also have to follow the instructions as to when to move forward, stop, etc.

One bright sunny day a priest with a van full of nuns entered one of our car washes. The van was barely able to enter the wash. Then the machinery engaged and followed its predestined course. This course of predestination began to peel the roof off the "Van of Holiness."

"Baptismal Waters" bathed the prostrate, cleansing them to a purity they had never before experienced. Out of the "Van of Holiness" they stumbled and sputtered, hopefully uttering praises and not curses to the Lord. The "Van of Holiness" now bore a remarkable resemblance to an opened can of sardines albeit without "the little fishers of men."

* * *

I had not been promoted to the field training supervisor position very long when I stopped in one morning at the last store I had managed for a drink and a short visit. It was great to see my former employees. I knew that the day would be a good one as we chatted and updated our lives.

One of the cashiers suddenly turned to me where I was standing on the side of the L- shaped checkout.

"Ms. Kathy, I cannot ring him up!" she whispered, indicating a nice-looking twenty-something man on the other side of the checkout.

"What is wrong?" I whispered back. I could not see any cause for alarm and both of his hands were visible to me.

"Please come and look," she whispered back.

Baffled, I went behind the checkout as she had requested. As I smiled at the young man, I then noticed that his pants were partially unzipped revealing neon red silk underwear with the tip of his erect penis poking out. What a salute to us group of women, none of whom were revealing their astonishment, embarrassment, amusement, or confusion to this early morning "greeting!"

Not to be outdone or outflanked by this "salute," I sweetly addressed the young man, "Sir, before I can ring you up I need for you to take care of the issue with your pants zipper."

To which he hastily replied, "Oh, oh, yes, ma'am," zipping and concealing his entertaining, silky, semi-clad salutation.

We all had a good laugh after he left and to this day when we refer to a "salute," it has a whole new meaning!

* * *

Even though inspections were highly stressful, every once in a while we managed to have some fun. One of the owners of the company was someone you could have fun with. He was always tough, but fair. He was respected, admired, and sometimes feared.

As field training supervisor, I was accompanying the Area Supervisor on inspection with the owner as lead inspector. It was in October and the stores were encouraged to celebrate the season. This particular store was decked out for Halloween with a vengeance.

As we all approached the entryway, we came upon a full-sized, real, black wooden coffin. There were spider webs draped off the coffin stretching up to the columns supporting the gas island canopy. The owner looked at the coffin and turned to me and said, "You have to learn to watch out during this time of year as the stores love to scare us. Usually there is someone stuffed into these things." As he spoke, he gave the coffin a slight tap with his foot.

The coffin sprang to life spewing forth a realistic vampire complete with fangs dripping blood and a ghastly white face! We all instinctively gasped and jumped back! I then realized that this was not a fake dummy but one of the employees who I knew well!

You could tell that the owner, even though startled, loved it. All of the employees inside the store were also in costume. They made sure to give us candy and we found it hard to be very critical of any small store issues that we discovered during our inspection.

* * *

When I became a supervisor, I had difficulty learning to delegate responsibility. I can remember being told, "You can manage eight people. You can't manage eight stores." I had to depend upon my store managers to give me accurate, unbiased information; in short, the truth, as they best could determine it.

One night around 9 p.m., I received a phone call from my store manager in Hazlehurst, GA.

"That sorry midnight girl just called out again. This is the second time this week. She claims she is too sick to work. You need to come fire her and hire me someone I can depend upon. I am sick and tired of covering these shifts."

"Why are you so sure she isn't sick?"

"They are never sick. They are just sorry. Besides I just watched a tape on her from two nights ago and all she did was sit behind the checkout. She didn't do hardly any of her side work."

The next morning I arrived at the store to a very tired and irate store manager who continued to rail about the midnight girl. This girl had been there for several years (longer than I had been in my position in the area) and had always been a good and loyal worker. I had never met the girl, so I had to rely on my store manager's opinion. We tried to call the girl to have her come in and meet with me. We could not get an answer. By the time I left the store, my manager had convinced me to fire her and look for another employee.

Less than two hours later, I got a call from a different store manager in the same town. She had just heard that EMTs had been called to this midnight girl's home where she had been found unresponsive. She had been taken to the hospital, diagnosed with pneumonia, and died of kidney failure by the end of the day. I felt such shame and anger at myself for assuming that my store manager's information was factual and accurate. I had failed to dig deeper.

Never again did I take any of my store manager's opinion on terminating an employee without first doing a thorough investigation of the circumstances. While I needed their input, I learned to get as many facts as I could to reach the truth that at times can be so elusive.

* * *

One of the things we were required to do as Area Supervisors was to do quarterly night rides. You showed up unannounced during the midnight shift and did a mini-inspection. The purpose of these night rides was to make sure you stayed on top of your area as well as demonstrating to your employees that you were unpredictable and that any nefarious goings on should not be attempted by them.

When I came into the store, Music had a friend at the end of the checkout counter with whom he was carrying on a conversation. I introduced myself and went about my business. Music was young, white, and looked unkempt with his scraggly hair and wrinkled shirt. Sort of a scruffy, hippie look. Definitely not the preppie type but midnight shift people are in a class all their own (since I started out as one I could vouch for that). People who work midnights have a multitude of reasons why they find themselves on third shift.

Music assured me that his friend was going to leave shortly (company policy only allowed for friends and family to "hang out" for 15 minutes). I finished up and left.

I visited the other two stores in town. I then decided it might be a good idea if I revisited Music to see if the friend had left. This was about two hours later. Well, Music's friend was still there and was happily munching on a Dandee sandwich. As soon as I walked in they both mumbled something, and the friend left.

The next day I went back to the store and pulled the video tape to watch Music's shift. Sure enough Music and his friend were enjoying a "grazing party." Grazing is the term used to describe employees and their cohorts eating and drinking without paying for the merchandise. I instructed the manager to watch a few more shifts on Music and document the amount of merchandise that was being consumed and get me a total. It seems that Music and his friend were satisfying their daily nutritional needs nightly as well as a few alcoholic beverages that they would take home with them. Needless to say, Music did not hear melodious words from us as he was removed from his "free feed trough."

* * *

I was very naive when I started with Flash Foods. I was soon to learn lessons about greed, addiction, manipulation, and deception.

One of my managers was an extremely capable woman with many years of experience. She was highly esteemed within the company. However, she was not what she appeared to be.

Her store had been experiencing inventory shortages that were very significant. Given the fact that she had a stable crew and her stellar reputation, something was just not quite right. I had only been a supervisor for less than a year and had a lot to learn.

I investigated the usual stuff when I noticed a disproportionate number of voids in the store paperwork. I spent hours watching videos of these voids. It was a time consuming and tedious process. The evidence was overwhelming and conclusive. This company star of store management was falsifying voids and using the money to purchase lottery tickets.

I took my results to my District Manager. This was such a big deal that the manager demanded a meeting with the owners of the company. I had to show my documentation not only to her but to the owners. It was a nerve-racking experience. The video evidence was indisputable.

In my naiveté I asked if we could give her another chance. This was granted. Unfortunately, she repeated her theft in a more cunning way that was more difficult to unravel, but I was still able to discover and prove her theft.

She was terminated and avoided prosecution by reimbursing the company for the theft. I never again asked to keep a thief and I learned how powerful lottery addiction was.

* * *

The survival of the human species demands that we procreate. It demands that we procreate no matter the circumstances, obstacles, or social mores. This ability to be able to perform our duties as to procreation is quite astounding.

One early morning one of my fellow supervisors received a distress call from a local Baptist preacher. The call was most unpleasant as the supervisor was charged with harboring vile, perversions in the workplace.

It seems that the preacher had been out on a hospital call and had visited one of the supervisor's stores during the wee hours of the night. When the preacher came into the store, he was unable to locate any employees. He headed to the cooler to find a suitable cold beverage and as he reached for this beverage he was treated to a display of two humans indulging in what he deemed was sexual perversion. If you think about it, this is quite remarkable. Indulging in oral sex while in a frigid environment one cannot help but be impressed with their tenacity. However, the preacher was not impressed. He was a righteous servant of the Lord, and he did not find live-action pornography to be suitable for our company to allow. This was an outrage and an abomination!

I never did find out how this supervisor wrote this one up. I was just very happy that I did not have to do the paperwork!

* * *

On another night ride I headed to one of my tougher stores. Having started with Flash Foods as a midnight person, I was determined to know my people and not be some faraway company big shot who did not care about the world of the third shift. I knew firsthand that this shift was challenging, not only because you had to try to sleep during the day, but because of your well justified fear of being robbed or killed. One lesson that I had already learned was that while the manager was the key to a successful store, a dependable, honest, third shift was just as important. I had a special affinity for third shifters.

Anyway, I went on my first night ride to my "hood store". It was a Friday night. Let me tell you, it is a whole lot different after midnight than during the day. Before I set foot in the store I was propositioned at least four times, listened to comments about my nice ass, did I have an "Old Man," and if I did, why was he letting me out at night, as well as various selling points offered regarding the genitalia of these individuals. I could not help but laugh as I decided to accept these as compliments and not insults. After all I was in my late 40s, so I figured; enjoy the attention while it lasts.

***

It was a bright, sunny Saturday afternoon as I drove past Contrary's store. I had been working at some of my other stores but did not have plans to visit this one. There were several police cars parked out front. Clearly, I needed to stop and see what was going on.

Contrary and a police officer were in the back room rummaging through stacks of milk crates filled with old paperwork. Contrary was a pack rat, and it nearly took an act of God to get her to throw anything out.

Suddenly Contrary said, "Here it is. He was not lying." In the milk crate stashed in the middle of mounds of paperwork was a handgun. The officer took the gun, finished up his report, and left the store.

It seems that just prior to my arrival a local thug had run into the store with another thug in hot pursuit. The first thug yelled at Contrary to call the cops, "He's got a gun!" Both ran into the back. Contrary called the cops and was able to get them both to leave.

So, in the future when I would go to Contrary's store and "encourage" her to help me clean out her back room I would tell her we needed to make sure she was not stashing weapons for the locals.

***

When we conducted our required monthly cash audits of each store, one of the duties involved the dropping of the safe. The safes were under the checkout counters and the easiest way to drop was to sit on the floor. This was about a 30-minute process. Sometimes I was not visible to customers as they came up to the checkout. Sometimes they would give the cashier on duty strange looks since it appeared the cashier was having a conversation with an imaginary friend!

On one such occasion I was busy dropping. I was not visible at all to the customer. The only people in the store were me, my assistant manager, and one male customer. I was zoned out, barely aware of what else was going on until I heard, "Naughty Nally, Naughty Nally." What? What did he just say? Hm.

About that time Nally said, "Shush you!" I kept my head down and pretended ignorance.

The customer left. I looked up to see Nally, face flushed a brilliant, rosy, fluorescent red looking back at me!

Well, we just had a good laugh and I said, "Well, Nally, maybe one day you can tell me all about, Naughty Nally!"

* * *

The phone rang at 1:30 a.m. I always had a surge of adrenaline when I got middle of the night calls knowing that one rarely receives pleasantries at this hour unless it was from drunken friends who somehow thought you would be happy to hear from them.

"Ms. Kathy, sorry to wake you but I just sold all of the dirty books to some guy, and he paid with a credit card."

Hmm.

"So how much was the total purchase?" I asked.

"$1600.00 more or less."

"Holy shit!" bolted out of my mouth.

"The transaction went through, and everything seemed in order."

"Alright. I will follow up during normal business hours and hope this is not some kind of a scam."

That morning I went to the store and followed up. All was legitimate, so I did not have to answer for some kind of credit card fraud. Then I started receiving phone calls from my other store managers in that area. It seems that this same man had gone to every convenience store in the area, not just our company, but all stores that sold dirty books and bought each and every one of them. Clearly there was a bigger story out there on why he had done this. We were no strangers to the issues that selling pornographic material posed for us. The magazines were behind the checkout and if you wished to buy one, you had to get the cashier to get it for you.

Later in the day, I talked to law enforcement about the purchases and discovered the why behind all of this. A local church had been conducting a revival. Some prankster decided it would be funny to place pages from dirty books into the hymnals and bibles in all of the pews. It "revived" all who came. Needless to say, while this did wake everyone up, not everyone enjoyed the "biblical visions of the Garden of Eden." The man who had bought all the books was a member of this church.

The church later conducted a book burning and began to lobby for the removal of all pornographic materials in the area. For several years we did not sell dirty books in that area but eventually they did make their way back.

* * *

The voice on the other end of the phone began with a complaint.

"You are charging too much."

"Sir, what are we charging too much on?"

"Your midnight girl is overcharging."

"What product is she overcharging on?"

"For blow jobs in the back room."

What??!! in the world was he talking about? Was this some kind of a prank? I resolved to remain professional and dignified.

"Sir, I do not know what you are referring to. We try to have the best pricing amongst our competitors."

"Well, you better get her to lower her prices then."

"Sir, how much is she charging you?"

"She is charging $30.00. That is $5.00 too much."

"Thank you, sir, for bringing this to my attention. I will look into this."

I hung up and immediately called my store manager.

"I need you to watch surveillance video and see if your midnight girl is doing blow jobs in the back room. I just had a guy call me and complain about her charging too much!"

Well, it did not take long to confirm the fringe sales going on in the back room. So once again we were without a midnight shift. She had been a really good worker too. What a shame.

***

Once upon a time in the "Olden Days," convenience stores kept counter displays full of cigarettes. Cigarette companies paid a monthly fee for us to keep these out. They had to be kept full and placement on the counters was dictated strictly by a marketing department planogram that would be negotiated yearly with the cigarette companies. Operations (those of us who had to run the stores) hated them. They were heavily shoplifted, and we had a budget to keep.

One of my stores was having a bigger issue than most regarding the cigarette counter displays. The manager and I began to watch video tapes and focused on the displays.

The busier the store, the greater the opportunity for shoplifting, so we picked a Friday night tape and began to watch. The checkout line was long, and the displays were very handy. A hefty woman in a sweat suit captured our attention. First off, it was August. Why was she wearing a sweat suit? She was in line with a can of soda. As she came to the displays we were in for a "Treat." First, she pulled her sweat suit pants open and then began to stuff packs of cigarettes into her drawers. Packs of cigarettes slid down into her pants legs as well. She then opened her sweat suit top, and we were "Treated" to a show of breasts that were rapidly engulfing multitudes of cigarette packs. She had stuffed at least two cartons of the packs by the time she got to the register to be rung up. She paid for her can of soda and waddled out of the store!

I contacted the local detective to see if he recognized her. He took one look at the tape and said, "That is Heavy D."

"What?"

"She is a well-known shoplifter here. One time she even shoplifted a turkey from the IGA by putting it between her thighs and walking out the door. She was wearing a "Sunday Go to Church" dress. She can carry a twelve pack of beer with those thighs as well."

"A twelve pack?" I tried to envision this event. Just thinking about it I was chagrined to feel a small touch of awe and admiration for Heavy D's "Thunder Thighs."

* * *

The phone rang at 1:30 a.m., never a good time to get a phone call. In the convenience store business, it usually means a robbery has occurred. This call was from my District Manager. He said, "Kathy, do you have any spare cash registers?" I am half-awake thinking, is he drunk or something, calling me at this hour and asking me if I have any spare cash registers!? We usually kept spares in some of our stores as well as in our company vehicles. I replied, "Yes, I have one in my vehicle and also at a store in Hazlehurst."

"That's good since you need to go to Hazlehurst. Someone just stole their cash register," was his laughing reply. That is just great I thought.

I arrived at the store 30 minutes later to find the cops questioning my third shift employee, John, a colorful, no-nonsense man who was incredibly faithful, albeit not one to get in a hurry. One of the officers and I went to view the VCR tape of the incident.

The tape revealed that the minute John went into the cooler to stock it, a small, skinny black man rushed into the store, holding a jacket in front of him.

The door buzzer went off to alert John in the cooler that a customer had entered the store. Remember that John does not get in a hurry. In less than one minute the man wrapped the jacket around the cash register from the front of the checkout, ripping it off the counter, tearing loose the electric plug in it, and racing out the door with it. John comes out of the cooler, saying "Can I help you?" to an empty store. He then strolls to the door looking at the knocked over Cookies and Cream display that had gotten in the way of the thief. John went to the door, looked up and down the street, before turning back into the store. With both hands on his hips, he began to mutter to himself. He started to pick up the Cookies and Cream items, as well as a cigarette counter display that had been sitting right next to the register. He put all of these items on the counter where the register had been. He didn't notice the cash register was gone.

As he tidies up, a customer came in to pay for $4.00 worth of gas. John went around the counter to ring him up. "Well, damn. I ain't got no register!"

It was all the officer and I could do to contain our laughter. The thief took less than a minute to steal the register, while John took more than four minutes to see what had really happened!

* * *

The company was very generous and sponsored a yearly trip for upper-level management. One trip for the women and one for the men. One year the women went to Daytona Beach. We would leave on a Thursday and return that Sunday.

We had carpooled so that we had four or five women in each vehicle. Our trip was going to take about four hours. We always began to behave somewhat badly as soon as the vehicle was cranked up. This sometimes meant adult beverages for the passengers. The driver was always sober.

We came to a midpoint and stopped for gas and a bathroom break. There was a lot of riotous laughter going on but so far we had not embarrassed the company. We would always tell people that we worked for our competition in case we messed up somehow.

We loaded up as our driver searched in her purse for the keys. Hmm. No keys. She got out and looked under the seat. No keys. She then retraced her steps into the store, to the bathroom etc. No keys. Hmm. We were tempted to ask the store personnel if we could view their surveillance tapes to see what had happened to the keys, but we were pretty sure that we would be refused. The search continued for 45 minutes. The driver finally said that she was giving up and would use the spare key that she had attached under her license plate, something that many of us did.

We arrived at our hotel and checked in. We were booked four to a room and our driver was in a room across from the one I was in. Everyone decided to get into our bathing suits and head to the beach and bar. As I came out into the hotel hallway, I heard a bunch of screeching and laughing from the room across from mine. What in the world?

Seems that when our driver changed into her bathing suit her lost keys came tumbling out of her bodacious bosoms!

*   *   *

The call came just after 11 p.m. I had an armed robbery. A white man in a mask, carrying a shotgun, robbed my two female employees. They were terrified. There had also been one customer in the store when the store was robbed. The gunman had ordered him into the cooler. I did my best to comfort my girls, knowing that they were probably going to quit. I could not blame them one bit. Both were single mothers trying to raise their children, something that I could relate to.

The video had recorded the robbery and as we watched it with the police, there was one amusing tidbit in the midst of all the terror. The customer who had been ordered into the cooler was a small black man. The cooler he had been ordered into had a handle on the inside of the main metal cooler door that to the inexperienced eye did not appear to look like a handle. When the robber left the store, this man found his way out of the cooler by removing the gallons of milk (these were on the bottom shelf), pushing open the glass doors and then crawling out onto the store floor!

I felt awful that he had such a terrible experience, so I offered to take him home. He refused my offer stating instead, "We been robbed! I need some rock! I need some money for some rock!" Rock is just street slang for crack cocaine, and I was not about to feed his drug habit. I tried again to convince him to let me drive him home as this store closed at midnight and I hated to think of him outside in the dark so soon after this unnerving experience. My manager, a savvy black woman, said, "Just let him be, Ms. Kathy. He will be alright." So, I drove her home and then headed to the house.

When I opened the door to my house the phone was ringing. It was 911 again. The store had another alarm. What in the world?? I was thinking. I called the store. My manager answered. "No need to come back, Ms. Kathy. That man waited until we left, then got a brick and tried to break into the store. He probably wanted to steal some cigarettes to swap for some crack."

Poor guy. First, he finds himself trapped in a frigid cooler, now he was going to find himself in the "Hoosegow."

* * *

It was during the holidays, and we always seemed to be short of employees during the season. One store was so shorthanded that I realized I needed to work a shift for my manager who had been pulling several doubles and needed a break. So, one Sunday morning I opened up for her and began the day.

Sunday mornings are usually very quiet and slow compared to the rest of the week. I was moving along nicely with the paperwork and cashing out customers in between. This store was in a rough area of town and had some very interesting clientele. Some of them I even knew by name.

One of the regulars, a personable "Lady of the Night," came in as she was winding down her busy night. She had a few items, and we made some small talk as I rang them up.

She then proceeded to pluck her payment money from deep inside her ample bosom. Her money must have found a deep hiding place as she plundered through her breasts.

"There you are," she said as she plopped out a wad of bills onto the counter. Hmm. Along with the wad of bills was a plastic wrapper with some agricultural products inside. Hmm. "Oh, oh. Is that? Yes, it is, Kathy," I said to myself.

Shit. I was used to finding weed packets in the bathroom and on the floor from time to time but so far had not had to deal with the owner/owners of these agricultural products.

If I acknowledge the agricultural products, I will have to call the cops. I will have to show them the video tape and I will have to fill out an incident report.

I made change for the buxom "Lady of the Night" plopping it right on top of the agricultural products which she promptly snatched up and stuffed into the depths of her bosom.

I said, "Have a nice day, sweetie!"

She just smiled, waved, and blew me a kiss.

* * *

Life was never dull, and people were the reason why. One of the many colorful characters that I met was a regular, an elderly black man known to all simply as Mr. JD. He always wore a hat and dressed nattily. His glasses gave him an air of wisdom. His shoes were shined and looked very spiffy. He was a class act, always carrying himself with dignity. He had presence and wit.

One day he came into the store and immediately spied a man by the cooler. All at once he was berating this man, sporting both of his fists, and carrying on something terrible. This was most out of character for Mr. JD! All around the store they went with Mr. JD yelling and screaming at this individual who was holding his arms up to protect himself from Mr. JD's feeble but unceasing blows! "I saw you steal that meat out of my cooler!!" Mr. JD exclaimed. "You no good thief, I'll make you wish you was never born!!" He went on and on, around and around the store they went! Mr. JD was half the size of this "Meat Thief", but Mr. JD was not afraid nor in any mood to cease and desist. Mr. JD's hat even flew off! I had never seen him without his hat.

About this time a man came into the store with a rake. Mr. JD seized this rake from him and began to beat "Meat Thief" with it. Seems this man with the rake had been working with Mr. JD when Mr. JD saw "Meat Thief" enter the store. Around and around they went. Finally, "Meat Thief" managed to get far enough away from Mr. JD to escape out the door. Ha, ha, ha!!

Mr. JD looked around for his hat, strolled over and dusted it off, then placed it upon his head. He then calmly strolled out the door.

My manager said to me, "Hm, wish we had Mr. JD working here. Bet no one would steal from the store!"

***

His name was Mich and he was a self-proclaimed "Hurricane Man." This meant that he liked to drink "Hurricane," a very large can of beer. He drank this beer daily. Mich was a "store fixture". He would walk from his home every day (a trip of about 7 or 8 miles) and come to the store and hang out for several hours. When he had his birthday, we always bought him a cake and celebrated with him at the store.

We loved our Mich. My manager had known Mich his entire life and she said that he was fine until he went into the military and then he became crazy and needed medication. He was very sweet and harmless. He actually needed us to watch out for him since there were those individuals who would take advantage of Mich. He was big enough that no one would try to physically harm him, but he was easily parted with his money by those who used guile and other means to make sure he gave it to them. He received a monthly check. While his parents were alive, they knew to dole it out over the month to him to prevent him being conned out of it.

One day I came to the store to hear that we had to call the police to pick Mich up. It seems that someone had conned him into taking cocaine. He had come into the store in only his underwear singing and dancing, "I am Hurricane Man, I am Hurricane Man." Poor Mich. It was several weeks before we saw Mich again. He was back to his regular crazy, sweet self! Thank goodness! We were so happy to see him at "his normal!" We bought his lunch and celebrated having our favorite "store fixture" back where he belonged!

* * *

One of the owners of Flash Foods was tough but fair when he inspected stores. Contrary was mischievous and loved to try and see if she could pull one over on him.

I had great respect for Contrary. She was like your favorite Drill Instructor. She could cuss and raise hell with the best of them. The clientele at her store were street savvy, demanding, and would brook no nonsense, smelling phonies a mile away. They also respected Contrary. No one could run this store like Contrary. Before she had taken over, it was an unmanageable den of iniquity. Once she got there it became a manageable den of iniquity. Contrary taught me how to document video tapes for prosecuting theft. The judges knew when she brought evidence to court it was solid and conclusive, making their job easier. She was a Flash Legend.

The only issue I did have with Contrary was that she was a pack rat. She never threw anything away when it came to old paperwork, etc. I decided that to encourage her and some of my other managers, I would devise a monthly contest to rid my stores of old paperwork and junk.

I found a large rubber rat at Walmart during the Halloween Season. He was pretty grotesque with a revolting snarling face and was posed on his hind legs with his two front paws clawing at you. He was very creepy and disturbing. I would leave this "Pack Rat" at whichever store had the most egregious junky cabinets at that store for one month in an effort to shame the manager to clean the cabinet out. Pictures were taken to document the shame of receiving the Pack Rat Award.

Contrary won the Pack Rat Award. She did not give a shit. The junky cabinets were still junky a month later with said "Rat" still in his JUNK NEST. Inspections were up coming. I left the "Rat" with Contrary.

The day of inspection, the owner was opening drawers, wiping his hands on shelves, and looking for cobwebs or any other cleanliness issues. He went to the fountain machine to check the nozzles for mold. All was clean and sparkling. Then he bent down to open the cabinet under the fountain. As he pulled the cabinet doors open he screeched and jumped back as "Rat" sprang out, paws with claws reaching for him!

Contrary had taken elaborate pains to make sure he would think twice about looking into her junky cabinets!!

***

We all tend to stereotype the kind of people who commit robberies. They must all be worthless, violent thugs who care nothing for the rest of humanity. I discovered that this could not be further from the truth after one of my stores was robbed.

It happened during the wee hours of the morning. I got the call and headed to the store. My employee told me she was fine, just scared and shaking. She was holding it together pretty well and said she would be back. She did not quit. I so admired and respected her. Would I have been able to do the same? I doubted it.

The video showed the robbery in good detail, including most of the conversation. What I remember vividly was the statement the robber made, "I know you; I know where you live, and I will kill you." He told her this repeatedly while he pointed his gun at her.

As the investigation unfolded, a witness from a business next door provided a vital clue. He had spotted a car parked in the back alley that had distinctive flashy wheels on it. A day or two later, the police pulled over this very vehicle and arrested the robber. Evidence was also uncovered at his apartment that he shared with his infant child and girlfriend. He was in his early twenties.

One of the detectives working the case came and collected the rest of what he needed from me and revealed a heart-rending twist to the whole wretched business.

The robber was a young black man who had never been in trouble. He had been working on a factory line, making a decent living, and had just recently bought the car with the flashy wheels. Then he had an epileptic seizure at work. He was terminated. I suppose that they were concerned about his seizures since it was a factory line he was on. The robber was unable to find work. It seems no one was willing to chance hiring an epileptic. He was about to be evicted from his apartment. No place for him, his girlfriend, or new baby to live. He made the choice to get his rent money by robbing the store.

Never again have I thought in terms of black and white when a crime was perpetrated in my stores. What was the story? What was the human element? How terrible it must be to reach this point of desperation. But most of all, I felt shame for having been so judgmental.

* * *

At one time or another two of my three children worked for Flash Foods. One summer my daughter, Loralei, worked in one close to home while taking organic chemistry at Middle Georgia College. She was not yet 21, so Flash Food policy required that she work with another employee to reduce the possibility that she might be tempted to sell alcohol to underage friends. This meant she would not be able to work midnights, something I was grateful for, since third shift was almost always single shifted. No mother wants her child working midnights in the "Shop and Rob" industry.

The store where Loralei worked was a high-volume store in a small middle Georgia town. The area had plenty of meth heads, alcoholics, and ladies of the night mixed in with churchgoers, politicians, and educators. Some even had teeth. Some even attended the local college. In other words, your average, small, Georgia town.

The second time she worked she was put on the three to eleven shift. This is the busiest shift in most stores and is usually double shifted. I had gone to bed around nine. Sometime after midnight I heard her come in the door. She walked back to my bedroom and said, "You must really love us to work for these people!!" She then stomped back to her room and slammed her bedroom door!

Nothing like a little reality check to keep your children in college! I would always have a ready "MOM SAYING" when any of them talked about dropping out. "Well, you can always find work in a convenience store!" HA!

* * *

One of our more amusing tales involved an incident in a tiny bathroom. This bathroom was more of an afterthought and the only one in the store. This bathroom had been installed before you had to have ADA compliant bathrooms. It was so small that one had to back into the toilet space and then take your position.

Adjacent to this store were a number of trees that were populated by a community of very cute squirrels. You know the kind. The ones you would just love to cuddle, snuggle, and squeeze. They loved to run around on the roof of the store, jumping from their respective trees, chattering, or stuffing their cheeks with squirrel foodstuffs. They were very entertaining.

On a bright sunny day a rather large lady made her way to the tiny bathroom. The clerk nervously watched as she closed the door. He knew all too well the logistics that would be involved in her visit. There was the possibility that her backing up endeavor might not be successful.

For a few minutes all seemed well. Perhaps he had misjudged her ample bottom width. Perhaps it was an optical illusion he was suffering from and there would not be a frantic call to 911 for a crew to remove said "Lady Large."

All of a sudden there were some thudding noises from the bathroom followed by a hysterical shriek! The bathroom door was rocking and the shrieks and thudding increased. The clerk rushed to the door and tried to open it, but it was blocked by "Lady Large." He could hear blows to the walls of the tiny bathroom. Just as he was about to call 911 "Lady Large" burst out from the door with her panties billowing around her ankles. As she ran screaming from the store he was horrified to find a squirrel trying to swim out of the toilet!

He looked up and saw that the ceiling tile had been nudged aside and evidently the squirrel had fallen into the toilet about the time that "Lady Large" had been backing into toiletry position!

Just then the "Swimming Squirrel" managed to escape his toilet pool, ran out between the clerk's legs, and proceeded to plunder the store. He went leaping from shelf to shelf, knocking over displays and sending boxes of products crashing to the floor. Customers were running all over the place and mayhem reigned. Some customers were even screaming, "Rabid squirrels, rabid squirrels!" This went on for some time until finally our undaunted maintenance man bravely captured and released into the wild the cute, cuddly, snuggly, toilet swimming squirrel. After all, surely he would never again venture into the attic roof again after the vision of loveliness he had been subjected to.

* * *

Once I was drafted to conduct a division night ride in an area other than my own. It was within driving distance of my own division, and I actually was looking forward to visiting stores other than my own, thinking that I could learn something that might help me improve my division.

I made my way from one store to another. This was a small town, and our store was a major shopping destination. It was always very busy and had a Subway inside it as well.

One required duty of the night ride was counting the registers. There was a company policy that allowed no more than $100.00 in each register. Clerks had what is called a drop safe that allowed the clerk to drop money as well as buy change from this safe. The manager was required to make sure that the safe was secure and full of change to ensure safe operations in the store. Store robberies have been dramatically reduced with the advent of these safes since the clerks cannot open these safes. With only $100.00 in the registers, this deters robbers who want a better return on their "Robbing."

Imagine my horror when I counted over $1,600.00 in this store's register! When I questioned the clerk, he told me that there was no change in the safe, so he had to keep enough money in his register to be able to do business. I immediately notified the proper authorities so the manager could come and address the issue. She never arrived.

***

One of my managers had two girls. Her youngest, Ronni, was the most outgoing, fun child you could ever hope to meet. She was always laughing, and her laughter was contagious. The store was right next to her elementary school and every day after school Ronni came to the store to check in with her mother.

This particular afternoon, Ronni breathlessly came into the store trying to get her mother's immediate attention. She was definitely in a huff. "What is your hurry?" asked her mother.

"Mama that lady lied on me!" exclaimed Ronni. Ronni was not laughing nor smiling, she was upset.

"What lady?"

"My teacher lady!" Ronni anxiously stated as she handed her mother a note.

"Your teacher lady says you were talking and would not stop even when she told you not to."

"No, Mama, I was only moving my lips!"

Brouhaha! We all could not help ourselves as we tried to picture the loquacious Ronni moving her lips soundlessly!

I never did find out what punishment was doled out to Ronni unless she made her demonstrate "Lips Moving Soundlessly!"

***

Lala was a scrappy, witty, hardworking manager who always had her store in great shape. She could find the funniest things to say, and a day spent with her was filled with laughter.

One day I arrived around noon. She was ready to share an early morning event with me. It involved a customer who apparently felt entitled enough to take all of our creamer and sugar packets from the beverage center. He was doing this on a daily basis, and it had become an issue. His pockets overflowed and sometimes these condiments fell out onto the floor. Keep in mind that we had a budget to meet, and in recent years some customers would abuse the free condiment perk and take them home for personal use instead of just using what was necessary for their drink purchase. These few apparently had no shame.

Lala had spoken to him on several occasions trying to get her point across without embarrassing him or insulting him. This had no effect on him at all. This morning she told him that his excess was going to have to result in a .25 cent fee. His reply, "Fuck you, bitch!" He then threw his hot cup of coffee at her and stomped out of the store!

Lala smiling replied, "You too, sir! Have a nice day!"

I wonder to this day if he ever got what she really said!

* * *

Everyone loved Sweet Thing. An attractive, feisty, outgoing black woman, she knew everyone. Any day you got to spend with Sweet Thing was a treat. I was privileged to be her boss for a time; a time that enriched and broadened my life.

One day as I was working at her store, she told me a story about Champale. Champale is a malt beverage that we sold.

A young white guy was perusing the selections in the alcohol section of the cooler, furtively glancing at Sweet Thing as she waited on customers. He finally made his way to the checkout and put a soda on the counter for her to ring up. He was squirming somewhat suggestively below the waist. Sweet Thing, noticing his squirms says, "How about that Champale in your pants?"

He replies, "What Champale? All I have is this soda."

Undeterred, Sweet Thing points to a large bulge behind the zipper in his pants, "That Champale."

He boasts, "That's just me."

To which Sweet Thing, hands on her hips, states unequivocally, "Ain't no white man built like that. Put that Champale up here and pay for it."

Still in denial he shakes his head no. Sweet Thing, not to be out done, comes from around the counter, reaches into his pants and retrieves the Champale.

As she related this story I asked her if she thought there might be health department repercussions if we sold "pant retrieved Champale." To which she revealed, "I put it in the out of dates and the vendor picked it up."

* * *

Sweet Thing had an uncle that everyone knew as Uncle Bookie. He had some issues and needed medication but was known to be harmless. Everyone understood how he was and accepted him. He was a store fixture.

Stores are regularly inventoried. Sweet Thing's store always had great counts. One day the count was significantly short. We could not account for around $500.00 in merchandise. We poured over figures, researched credits, and looked at new employees on video until we were exhausted. Nothing. We were stumped.

Later that night, worn from the day's events, Sweet Thing went to her mother's for dinner. Her mother, unaware of the shortage at the store, told Sweet Thing that everyone in town was buying dirty books from Uncle Bookie. This was not well received by Sweet Thing's mother as she and the entire family were very active in the church. Just imagine, a member of the family out selling porn. Disgraceful, even if he was somewhat intellectually compromised.

Immediately Sweet Thing knew where those dirty books had come from. She recalled that the magazine credits had been in a box behind the checkout. She had assumed that they had been picked up, per policy, and credited. Back to the store she went to watch more video, focusing on the box full of dirty books. Somehow this box had not gone back to the vendor. Uncle Bookie had "booked" with the nasty books! It seems that he was such a fixture that no one had paid any attention when he picked the box up and left the store!

***

Sweet Thing had a fear of dogs. This fear seemed irrational to me. I told her upon more than one occasion, "Your ancestors hunted lions with only spears. I do not understand your fear of dogs, which are insignificant morsels of food to lions. Your ancestors lived with all kinds of wild beasts and dealt with them accordingly. We white people only had to deal with some bears and mountain lions which pale in their terror in comparison." She would say, "Well, maybe there is some white blood in me." We would just laugh.

One night she came to spend the night with me before we had a supervisor meeting the next day. We were to meet at a store so she could ride with me to my home. While I was at the store waiting on her, the mother of the store manager called the store to ask if the manager was at the store. The mother had been calling her daughter for over an hour and the phone was busy, causing her to be concerned. I told the mother that I would drive by her house and check it out and have her call. Sweet Thing arrived and we headed to the manager's on the way to my house.

Sweet Thing asked me if there were any dogs. I said, "Yes, one, but she keeps it leashed or inside." The dog was a huge Rottweiler. By now it was dark. We pulled into the driveway and made our way to the door of the house.

The door of the house opened, and this huge, black shadow of a monstrous dog came bounding out, barking, and heading in our direction. Sweet Thing shrieked and shinnied up the hood of my van onto the roof! I did not know she could move that fast! I felt terrible that this had happened to her and tried to reassure her. I had met the dog before and this had never happened.

Fortunately, the manager brought her snarling beast in control before anything more transpired. We found out that her son had been and was still on the phone with his girlfriend. No one had died or been foully murdered.

We got Sweet Thing off the roof of the van and headed to my home. I also had a dog. Katie was a very sweet and unintimidating black Lab that my son had rescued from the dump. I assured Sweet Thing that the dog would sleep in my son's room, and we would make sure that Katie did not have her usual run of the house until we left the next morning. Sweet Thing was in no mood for any dog, no matter the sweetness of temperament. She spent the night in the guest room with the chest of drawers pushed against the door in case of canine intrusions.

* * *

It was a boiling hot, humid August day in Kingsland, Georgia. Customers in that part of the world knew how to cope with the tropical, steamy weather. We were constantly amazed as well as revolted by some of the "Summer Wear." Mounds of flesh that would be tastefully hidden in the two winter months of January and February were revealed in all their sweaty, pungent, blubbery grotesqueness. This was not the case the rest of the year. Evidently mirrors were in short supply during the hot months. Or perhaps fat was just in fashion.

On this occasion, the customer in question was not fat but he was hot. Into the air conditioned store he strode. He went directly to the ice box. He did not waver. He did not allow himself to be distracted. As he negotiated his journey around displays and aisles he began to shed his clothing. By the time he reached the ice box he had "Flashed" his white and shiny birthday suit for all to see. He opened the door to the ice box and crawled inside, positioning himself in a comfortable pose on top of the bags of ice. The only statement he made was "It's really hot."

It was times like these that we often remarked about our company name, Flash Foods. Evidently our customer believed in one of our mottos, "Flash People, Together We're Better."

* * *

We had a mystery. It seems we were missing some of our "Adult Magazines." These were kept behind the checkout so shoplifting should not have been the cause. It had to be either employee theft or some shenanigans by way of the vendor.

We were short staffed, so we were not up to date on viewing VCR recordings. We needed to focus on watching the "Adult Magazines" and see where they were traveling to. I had just about decided that I would have to take some tapes home and view them myself when I received a call from the store manager.

"There is a problem in the back room. We had a customer who was on his way to the bathroom suffer some minor injuries. He has gone to the hospital to get checked on."

"What?"

"I can't really explain it. You need to come to the store and see it for yourself."

Hmm. Intrigued I made my way to the store and followed my manager to the back room.

The backroom floor was littered with a mass of "Adult Magazines." These had fallen upon the bathroom bound customer. What in the world?

My manager tapped me on the shoulder and pointed up.

The ceiling tiles in the middle of the back room had broken, allowing the rain of "Adult Magazines" to cascade onto the ill-fated customer below. Now who had put these in the ceiling? We now knew where the "Adult Magazines" had traveled to but still needed to find the "Human Connection."

My manager was so happy that the "Adult Magazine" mystery was solved she pulled all her VCR tapes and watched until the rest of the mystery was resolved. Seems a certain clerk was filling in the slow times late at night with an out of the camera's reach studious reading in the backroom. He was seen going putting a sign on the door "Back in 5 minutes." Next, he took a magazine and disappeared into the netherworld of the backroom. There he would remain for around 5 to 7 minutes. He then returned, but the "Adult Magazine" did not.

Now, how does one write up the necessary paperwork?

Customer injured by foul creatures attacking customer with foul books?

Customer injured by spirits of deceased Puritans offended by blasphemous, heinous literature?

Only the Shadow knows.

* * *

It may defy all logic, but one would assume that if a video camera is recording your every move and conversation, one would behave with discipline and professionalism. This is not always the case.

There was a Flash Tale that concerned an uproar between a store manager and her assistant manager. It seems that the tape told a tale that could not be denied.

One duty of management required viewing video tapes as a proactive means to prevent employee theft and ensure professional behavior in the workplace. This manager pulled a tape to watch and found less than professional behavior. On this particular tape, her assistant manager was pulling a midnight. Around 2 a.m., in walks the manager's husband. The assistant manager goes over to the monitor and turns it off. This action only turns the video feed off on the monitor. It does not stop the recording.

What ensued was an X-rated porn scene behind the checkout. The well-nourished assistant manager and the scrawny manager's husband provided astonishing acrobatic displays of a sexual coupling that established them as world class athletes.

This sort of behavior did not exactly fall into "Flash Food Business-like Professional Behavior." It also created a strain on the relationship between the manager and her assistant, becoming a "Human Resource Department Issue." We always dreaded "Human Resource Department Issues." It was certain to be determined that all of this could have been avoided had the assistant manager been properly trained in video operations!

* * *

Catching employee theft is not enjoyable to me. This hard reality of life was brought home to me in a gut-wrenching discovery.

I was researching inventory shortages at a store where the manager had often made accounting errors that would cause a nonexistent inventory shortage.

I felt sure that this time would be like all the others. I would take the time to teach my manager on how she created the error and hopefully avoid making the same mistake in the future.

I was scrolling through items on the store computer when all of a sudden I saw a pattern that I had never seen before. My heart began to thump, my head got hot and I blurted out, "Why are you storing tickets?"

I looked up into the eyes of my manager and I knew, I just knew. And she knew I knew. I then removed all of the video tapes from the store, replaced them with new ones, printed out the documents I needed from the computer and left to go home and validate what I knew in my heart. She had found a new way to steal. Our previous software did not have the functionality to store tickets. She was storing tickets and then after the customer left the store she would void the ticket and pocket the money.

The next day we were having a District Manager meeting. I had not yet finished my investigation, so my manager was still supposed to be at work. I would not confront her until I had the solid proof I needed. She did not show up at the meeting. I called her with no result. Her sister who managed another store for me was at the meeting and contacted the family who began to search for her. Later, after the meeting, her sister called me and said they had found her. She had tried to hurt herself.

***

If you think that human failings are a matter of black and white and easy to judge and categorize, you are dead wrong. All too often we exercise our judgment in a way that demeans and belittles the object of our scorn. The longer I stayed in my position of "someone's boss", the less judgmental I became. My position of authority and power became a burden and a responsibility, not something that I enjoyed or relished.

Not too long after I had to terminate and prosecute one of my best managers for theft, I received a phone call from the bank. The head bank teller told me that she needed to see me in person. Dread and a sickening feeling came over me. Please, not again. What was even worse, the store in question was managed by the sister of the manager I just had to terminate and prosecute-she had felt such shame she had tried to hurt herself. Both of these managers were extremely hard workers who put in long hours, never complained and were loved and treasured by the community. Surely the bank just had some accounting issue I would be able to unravel.

Well, there was some unraveling to do but it only revealed theft. The theft was clever and involved rolling money orders. I had never seen or heard of theft in this manner.

When there was theft, I was required to do a complete cash audit. Cash audits are routinely done once a month per store so when I went to the store and began my audit my store manager knew that something was up. I had already done this month's audit a few days before.

My store manager immediately confessed. She had bought a small truck from her brother. She was paying him the payments, and he was supposed to be making the payments as the truck was still in his name. He did not make the payments. He kept the money. The bank was going to repossess the truck leaving her without any means of transportation. Without any means of transportation she would not be able to get to work.

It was a really shitty day. I really liked her and her sister as well, yet here I had to do this shit thing again. I cared that she was going to lose her job and that she would now have a criminal record. Getting work again would be impacted by this. How I wish she would have come to me. But she didn't and now I just felt sick about the whole thing.

No, life is not about clear and easy judgments. It is about agonizing and painful decisions that impact peoples' lives.

* * *

Flash Foods believed in working hard but they also liked to party hard. At least before a new boss came on board. Once he came you had better not have too much fun or he would get rid of you.

We were having what was called a vendor outing which was code for the vendor paid to let you be a gluttonous, drunken pig should you so choose. I rarely drank at that time because I was responsible for stores that operated 24 hours, 7 days a week, 365 days a year. You did not go to a robbery if you were drinking. That meant that if you drank at all it only occurred at one of these outings.

There is an alcoholic beverage called Goldschlager. Horrible stuff it is. However, when an owner of the company offers this vile brew you accept and maintain a look of beatification upon its ingestion, glowing in the warmth and camaraderie that inspires professions of the goodness of the human spirit, "I love you man" to everyone you see. It is extremely potent with little flecks of gold in it. I am pretty sure that in my high school chemistry class we learned that metals are not all that good for you.

I began to feel somewhat funny in my stomach. I rarely vomit so if that was about to occur it would be a dreadful, foul thing indeed. I was swaying. Luckily one of our head honchos, a lovely woman named Geni took charge of me. "I love you Geni" I fuzzily managed to vocalize. Geni was our IT genius. She had also babysat the two owners when they were children and would often tell people that she "had slept with the owners!!!" She along with a few others who looked upon me with compassionate alarm guided me to my room.

Well, I can tell you today that no one in the entire company can state that they threw up on Geni. This is my claim to fame at Flash Foods. Even better, she has remained a dear friend in spite of it all!

I love you, Geni!

* * *

Every morning I would get up and run. I ran early, usually between 5:30 and 6:30. I ran all around town where one of my stores was located. I got to know the early morning people, most of whom were loyal customers.

One morning I was running when one of the regulars stopped me and said,

"Your store is not open yet." This store was supposed to open at 6 a.m. and close at 11 p.m.

So, I changed my route to run by the store. Yep, it was still closed and getting close to 6:30. I headed home to use the phone and call my manager. After several calls she finally answered the phone. "I have hemorrhoids and I am not coming in." Hmm. Okay…

"I will need the keys so I can open the store. Why didn't you call me to tell me you were not going to be able to open the store?"

"Didn't think you would find hemorrhoids a good reason to not open the store."

Well, there was no point in trying to get her to see how illogical her thinking was. I knew she also drank sometimes and wondered how sober she was.

I drove to the store, still attired in my running clothes as it was vital that I get the store up and running before I did anything else. I would just have to hope I was not too odorous for my customers.

She finally showed up with the keys around 7 a.m. Needless to say I was fuming but I kept it under wraps and hurried to open, get the paperwork done and call someone in to run the store.

So, the next time you go to your favorite early morning store for your coffee and snacks be happy that the clerks have showed up, hemorrhoids or not.

* * *

Ms. Bea was a jewel of a lady. Always dependable, always friendly, she was a joy to work with. She had grown children and grandchildren. I do not remember how many years she had been at Flash but they exceeded mine.

One night as she was working second shift in an 18-hour store that closed at midnight she was robbed. The robber hid his weapon in the loose shirt that he wore. She could not tell what it was, but we do not take chances; always give the robber the money. Do not tempt fate.

She was unharmed and appeared fairly calm as I did my robbery audit. The police brought a dog to the scene and he seemed to pick up a scent. As far as we could tell the robber had come on foot but there was some concern that he had simply parked away from the store and our cameras.

I told Ms. Bea that she could take as much time as she needed to recover from the trauma of being robbed but she said she would be better off coming in as scheduled the very next night. I also knew that she needed to work as several family members were now living with her. She was a real trouper, stating that years ago she had been robbed at gunpoint and that did not keep her from her work then, and it was not going to keep her from her work now.

Within the same week she was robbed again! As the police and I watched the video of the robbery we were astounded to hear Ms. Bea tell the robber, "You need to quit coming here and taking my money." What chutzpa!! She was kind of pissed!! Where was her fear?! I was not sure that was the best thing to say, however. What if the robber got mad and then shot her? You still could not tell what he held in his hand as he pointed it at her.

Again, she stated that she was coming to work. Nothing was going to deter her. I lived within two miles of this store and I ran every morning, in the dark, on the streets in and around the store, so I was also concerned about this robber in regards to my own safety. What if he decided to hit the store as it opened instead of late at night?

Just a few days after this second robbery the police broke the case. A teenager who attended the high school where my son did was arrested and charged. He lived only a few blocks from the store! He had a really nice family but unfortunately he had gotten into the drug scene and one thing led to another.

To this day I can still see Ms. Bea angrily telling this robber, "You need to quit coming here and taking my money!!"

* * *

As I came into the store I saw that my employees (all three were women) having a really good time laughing to the point of hysteria.

"So, this must be a good day today!"

"Oh, it really is, Ms. Kathy. It really is! Just wait until you hear about last night."

"That guy who stole the 12 pack of beer and went outside to wait on the cops didn't come back did he?"

"No, we think he is still in jail. Poor man, that was where he wanted to go. Told us he needed a place to stay. So, we guess he got a place. Last night's event was more interesting than that."

"Did you have to make out an incident report?"

"Well, that is just what we were trying to decide upon, so you need to tell us what to do."

"So, what happened?"

"Around 11:45 p.m., right when we were starting to close up for the night this guy comes in. He wanders around the store for a few minutes. We really wanted him to hurry up and get his stuff so we could ring him up and close. He finally comes up to the counter with some cookies. That was when we noticed that he was proudly displaying his penis for us to admire. We ignored his flaunted genitalia, rang him up and told him to have a nice night. But just as he strutted out the door we told him that he needed to take his penis home and grow it some more!"

Brouhaha!!

District Manager

When I became District Manager (DM) I was tasked with following up on any and all customer complaints in my district. The majority of customer complaints came into Corporate during the weekends, recorded for all posterity on a wave file. These were forwarded to each DM on Mondays. This gave birth to "THE WAVE FILE DILEMNA." Did I want to go ahead and listen to these rants, often full of bile and cursing, at the start of my day, or put them off until later? Many of these required that I return the call to the complainer while others I was able to delegate to the appropriate supervisor. If I started with them first I inevitably would alternate between apoplectic rage and hysterical, urine producing laughter. This would set the mood for the rest of the day. If I waited until closer to going home I would find my evening ruined as I raged against the necessity of being polite and professional to people who had clearly no idea of what civilized behavior was.

One Monday I began the day, cringing as I listened to one after another. One stood out as the most arrogant, snobbish, rude one of all time. It was a deeply offended, elitist, woman.

"I just want you to know that I had to go inside and prepay for my gas. This is the stupidest policy that I have ever heard of. Anyone with any common sense could see that someone driving a BMW is not the kind of person who drives off with gas. I am an attorney. I live on St. Simmons Island and that fat, son of a bitch that you have working for you should have known that I am not the type to drive off with your gas. You need to change your policy and train your people to recognize the differences in your customers so you can improve your customer service. I will not be shopping any of your stores again!"

So, we are supposed to train our people to recognize arrogant, elitist, snobbish, rich, bitches from the rest of humanity. Obviously, we are not worthy of visitation from this particular "SUPERIOR SPECIES" of the human race.

* * *

We would have store meetings to do training, build relationships and give employees a chance to voice their concerns. I welcomed suggestions that came from them. They had great insight on how to improve their store and I enjoyed attending these meetings. One of the best things about these meetings is that we always had fun. Everyone needs to have more fun! We tried to include food as well. Most everyone looked forward to our meetings. We did have a few Eeyores who did not like these meetings but not many.

At one store meeting the manager began with, "We have a problem with the Woodie Books." Hmm. I was trying to look smart and knowledgeable but in truth I had no idea what a Woodie Book was or why there would be a problem. All of the employees were looking at me, waiting for me to reply. Well, I had to come clean. I cleared my throat, "Um, what is a Woodie Book?" Everyone began to snicker. Some tried to hide their mirth in the crook of their elbows but before long the room erupted into shrieks of laughter. My supervisor was howling! Finally, the store manager said, "Ms. Kathy, Woodie Books are those dirty books that give guys a "Woodie." HA! So Woody Book is code for pornographic literature!! You can figure out what a Woodie meant.

It seems that the magazine racks where the Woodie Books were displayed allowed underage customers to see things on the covers that they should not see. Many mothers were voicing their concerns and making our company seem like purveyors of filth and lechery.

This turned out to be a very productive meeting and updated magazine racks were made available that allowed us to display the Woodie Books behind a cover that hid their risqué ladies in all their glory.

* * *

Sometimes we would have to deal with drugs being sold either in store parking lots or inside the stores. One incident was especially memorable.

I got a call from my supervisor that a drug deal had apparently been done during the middle of the night involving both the men's' and women's' bathrooms. The store had to close both bathrooms until maintenance could repair the damage. What in the world?

I arrived at the store and went back to the bathrooms which were located in the back of the store. It seems that the drug dealer had locked both bathrooms and then removed the ceiling tiles to go from one bathroom to the other without being observed on camera. I was amazed that the flimsy ceiling beams had been able to bear the weight of someone since they were only geared to hold up ceiling tiles. The ceilings and sinks had sustained enough damage that we could not allow usage until fixed.

* * *

One of the challenges you encounter when you move up the ladder is the misunderstandings between lower-level employees and Corporate. It is a major part of your job to try to humanize both levels so that everyone has a better understanding of the big picture. Low level perceptions include views that Corporate "Big Shots" are a bunch of self-serving, arrogant, loafs that have little or no respect for the hard work that the store level people perform. This was bought home to me on one of my first store inspections as a team leader. These inspections were held quarterly and figured prominently in both the store manager and assistant manager's bonus. It was an extremely stressful time for store people.

My team members, who were from Corporate, were to meet me the night before for dinner. We were out of town and on the company dime since the area we were to inspect was some distance. I was always careful not to abuse this privilege.

The two team members, a man and a woman, stayed at the restaurant after I left. They were consuming alcoholic beverages. We agreed to meet in the hotel lobby at 7:30 a.m. We were scheduled to being inspecting the first store at 8 a.m.

The next morning, they did not show up. I called each one of them repeatedly and had the desk clerk call their rooms. I did not get an answer. The desk clerk did not get an answer. I then had to try and figure out which rooms they were staying in. I was able to recall the one that the woman was in.

I knocked on her room. No sound. I then commenced to beat upon the door. She finally comes to the door. The room was dark and it was evident that I had woken her. She reeked of beer. I told her that I was leaving for inspection and I left to conduct the inspection alone. I had already called the area supervisor to tell her that we were running late. I was furious. I remembered how at store level I had come in around midnight to make sure my store was in tip top shape for the Inspectors. These two Inspectors had no consideration for the people in the stores.

I contacted their respective bosses. They later showed up as I was finishing the first store. They both were still very drunk. Their odor was horrible.

What so infuriated me was that during the night, while they whooped it up, the store people had been at work preparing to present an immaculate store. Some even worked the entire night.

* * *

On another occasion I was involved in documenting a worker's comp complaint. An employee said she had hurt her back while working in the cooler during the midnight shift. I viewed the security tape. This employee, in four days, never even went into the cooler to stock it, much less get injured.

* * *

It would be logical to assume that those in charge are competent, resourceful, organized, and intelligent. In other words, people who "Have Their Shit Together." This is not always the case.

After I became a DM I would make it a point to recognize my supervisors' birthdays. I would go to whichever store they were working at and break up the daily work routine by having a small celebration. It was a fun way to combine both work and pleasure.

When Sweet Thing's birthday came around, I contacted a fellow supervisor, Dee, who ran the area next to Sweet Thing's, to join me in surprising Sweet Thing with a cake, a small gift and lunch.

We met at the store and went to Sweet Thing's favorite restaurant to celebrate. We made sure to bring lunch back for the store employees. Dee needed to get back to her area and looked around for her purse. It was not in the store. It was not in my vehicle, in which we had ridden to go to lunch. It was not locked up in her van that we could see, although we had our doubts. Sweet Thing suggested that perhaps we should call the cops to unlock Dee's van to be sure. At that point in time, I was convinced that someone must have stolen Dee's purse from the store while we were at lunch. I angrily proclaimed, "We are going to go and watch the video and find the low life who stole your purse, Dee!" As we headed to the backroom to view the video Sweet Thing asked me, "Whose purse is on your shoulder?"

"This is your purse Sweet Thing; don't you remember giving it to me?"

At which Sweet Thing burst out laughing, "No, I do not carry a purse. That is Dee's!"

So here we are, the DM who oversees 61 stores, over 450 employees and millions of dollars in cash and inventory, two supervisors who are responsible for 7 to 8 stores each, 50 to 60 employees and millions of dollars in cash and inventory, running around like idiots looking for a purse that was on the shoulder of this supposedly competent, resourceful, organized and intelligent "Great Leader!" What a bunch of idiots we were!!!

Sweet Thing had the last word. "I am really glad we did not have to call the cops to break into Dee's van. Last week, at this very store, I had to call them to break into mine. As the cop and I walked over to break into my van I put my hand into my pocket to find a small device deep down inside. I spoke out loud, "What is this?" All of a sudden I realized that this device was my electronic clicker that opened my van! The look on his face revealed his sudden recognition that I was not entirely sane. You could see him thinking, "Ding Bat. I almost thought he was going to tell me to "Keep calm and I will get you some aluminum foil for your head to prevent the aliens from reading your thoughts!"

* * *

Since quarterly inspections stressed everyone out and that included me at every level I found myself in I tried to inject some humor and inspiration to the ordeals. I emailed a weekly update to my District and one of these emails included the story of Mike the Headless Chicken. First, this is a true story. In 1945 a farmer in Colorado was asked by his wife to go kill a chicken for dinner. Well, this chicken, as often happens, jumped up and ran around without his head. The farmer was unable to catch him so he beheaded a different one figuring he would find the first one in the morning.

The next morning he was astonished to find the headless chicken very much alive and pecking at the ground with his headless neck! He took the chicken and the head to a university where it was determined that enough of the brain stem remained with the chicken so he was still alive.

The chicken became known as "Mike the Headless Chicken". He was featured on the cover of Life Magazine. Mike lived 18 months. His owner fed Mike with an eye dropper. Mike thrived until he choked and died. There is a "Mike the Headless Chicken Festival" every May in Fruta, Colorado.

I emailed photos of Mike to my District and attempted to give them some comfort in this time of angst, "If Mike can live 18 months without a head you can get through Inspections!"

* * *

I kept Mike in mind a lot in the following years. The times that cars accidentally drove into stores narrowly missing customers and staff. ATMs were stolen in the middle of the night by people crashing a vehicle into the store, only to be unable to get the ATM out. There were "he said, she said" claims of sexual harassment that never seemed to be in view of cameras. No way to get to the truth was always frustrating. Sometimes, even years later, we would finally get to the truth. Kind of like your kids telling you the "Rest of the story" decades later. I said, "Oh shit!" a lot. Shit is a really great word. It sums up situations so succinctly and emphatically. Between Mike, "Oh shit" and my morning runs all was good.

And Then...

DECEMBER 29, 2016

"This will kill him."

Stunned, but unsurprised, my sister, Shelley, her daughter Marissa, and I, wept and shook.

I shoved my emotions into the abyss and asked, "How long does he have?"

"Maybe a year."

My voice from the abyss said, "We better make it count."

NOVEMBER 21, 2016

I was so excited! Doug was coming to spend Thanksgiving with me and my kids. He flew into Chattanooga from Tampa, arriving at 9:56 a.m. The drive to the airport from my cabin in Blue Ridge, Georgia, is about an hour and half. Our route took us through some of the most beautiful scenery in the north Georgia mountains, winding between the Ocoee River and towering mountain cliffs. The trees were still glorious in their fall finery. The weather was crisp and clear.

Doug loved his coffee. Like our mother, he always had a coffee in hand. His favorite was from MacDonald's, a "medium, four and four". This meant four creams and four sugars. When he visited I knew to make sure we went through the drive-through and order this brew. There was a MacDonald's just before we entered the scenic part of our drive and more than once we had made sure he got his "medium, four and four".

His plane was on time and I was so happy to see him. When we got close to the MacDonald's I said, "I will pay for your "medium, four and four". Your money is no good while you are with me."

But he declined. "Something is wrong with my stomach. I think I ate something that didn't agree with me. I better not have any coffee right now."

I did not think too much about this and continued to drive to the cabin.

I had purchased his favorite beer, Miller Lite. That evening we sat on the deck for a while then went inside to enjoy a cozy wood fire in the fireplace. He started to drink his beer but put it down after a few sips. He ate only a little of his meal.

"How long has your stomach been upset?" I asked.

"About two weeks. I think I got some bad chicken."

I remembered a time when I had food poisoning. It was almost a month before I felt normal so I just thought he might have the same thing going on.

NOVEMBER 22, 2016

I got up early and went into Blue Ridge for a run. Doug was up by the time I returned. I was scheduled to be interviewed at the cabin by a regional magazine about my book *Dear Dad*. Doug sat in on the interview. Sometimes he would make faces at me to try and get me to laugh. We still often acted like little kids.

Later we drove to the Book Exchange in Marietta and delivered some *Dear Dad* copies for the upcoming holiday sales. I had a special treat in mind for Doug. I took him to Semper Fi, a bar and grill in Woodstock owned and operated by two retired Marines, Ralph and Carrie Roeger. They cater to Veterans and first responders. It is filled with military artifacts, especially from the Marines. Doug was a Marine veteran, having served two tours. He had also served in the Army Reserves, making him a multiple military veteran. The names of menu items kept the theme of service going.

As I had hoped, he absolutely loved the place. He had a wonderful conversation with Ralph. We had a filling lunch and as we left we admired the truck with the logo of Semper Fi. Doug does not like to have his picture taken but he seemed to like posing in front of the truck from Semper Fi.

After lunch we headed to the movies and watched *Fantastic Beasts and Where to Find Them*. Then it was back to the cabin and a roaring fire.

NOVEMBER 23, 2016

We had a lazy morning before getting on the road to spend Thanksgiving in Spring Hill, Tennessee, where my oldest daughter Liberty and her husband Ryan were hosting the holiday. It can be a three and half hour drive or, on the eve of Thanksgiving, a five hour drive. The trees were brilliant still, and I had my best friend beside me. I was always so comfortable with Doug. We could talk or just ride in silence and it just felt so good. You know you are with someone special when you do not feel any need to fill up the silent spaces with talk.

NOVEMBER 24, 2016

Thanksgiving Day for us always begins with a Turkey Trot. Doug was still an excellent runner even though in recent years he had developed a knee problem. He ran cross country in high school and was the first one in our family to complete a marathon. After our trot we stopped by Starbucks and refreshed with our favorite caffeines, most with coffee, myself with a hot tea. Doug did not want anything.

We went with Liberty and Ryan to one of their friends' home for the main dinner. I could not help but notice that Doug did not eat very much and spent a lot of time outside on the porch. It was not unusual for him to keep to himself in social settings but there was something different about this. There were football games on and he loved football, yet he stayed outside alone. Clearly he was not himself.

Over the weekend we went to the musical, *The Grinch*. Doug was sick and going to the bathroom a lot. I was worried. My thinking was perhaps he had an ulcer or something.

We went home to my cabin and Doug enjoyed watching me put up Christmas decorations. He liked to tell me that there was an empty spot on the tree. Monday, November 28, he flew home to Tampa. He promised me he would go and see a doctor and find out what was wrong with him.

DECEMBER 1, 2016

I called Doug and asked how he was doing. I also wanted to confirm our upcoming trip to Tacoma, Washington. I had an upcoming book signing for *Dear Dad* at the Barnes and Noble in Lakewood, Washington and he was going with me. We were going to eat at some of our favorite restaurants that we always visited when our Dad was alive. We also were getting together with some old friends. It was a trip we were really excited about. He said he had an appointment with the VA and would let me know how it turned out.

DECEMBER 5, 2016

Doug called me and said that he could not go with me to Tacoma because the VA wanted him to come in on December 12. He had already bought plane tickets and I was disappointed and anxious that he would not be going with me. I would really miss him. And now I was worried. Today my Dad would have been 92. Somehow this bothered me.

DECEMBER 18, 2016

After numerous phone calls and tests, Doug was admitted to James A. Haley Veterans Hospital in Tampa. I put out enough food and water for my cat, Ninja, for three days and drove 560 miles to Tampa. Doug was unable to keep any food or liquids down. My sister and I were scared. No, we were terrified. All we knew at this point was that the testing had revealed a mass on his jejunum that was blocking his digestive processes. This meant there was going to be surgery.

Doug named his mass "Bob the Blob". I joked with him about a story he had told me about while he was in the Marines. He and another Marine were living off base and had enjoyed a night of copious amounts of adult beverages. Sometime in the early morning they were so hungry that they ate a package of bacon and they ate it raw. Ew. Trying to lighten the mood, I told him that he was going to be famous for having surgical removal of ancient raw bacon from his digestive tract.

DECEMBER 21, 2016

I drove back to the cabin and waited for news. There had been more tests and scans but so far no surgery. Doug was stable but still hospitalized, and I had to see about my cat. On December 23, Doug was released from the VA. He spent Christmas with my sister, Shelley, and her family. I went to my daughter Loralei's for the holiday. Originally Doug was supposed to have gone with me. It was an anxious filled time with little sleep. Not knowing what was ahead of us took all the joy out of the season. I just had dread. Dread when I woke up. Dread when I slept. Dread when I dreamed.

Doug was put back into the VA just after Christmas. On December 28 my sister called me, "They are doing surgery on him in the morning." I drove to Tampa in seven hours and forty-five minutes.

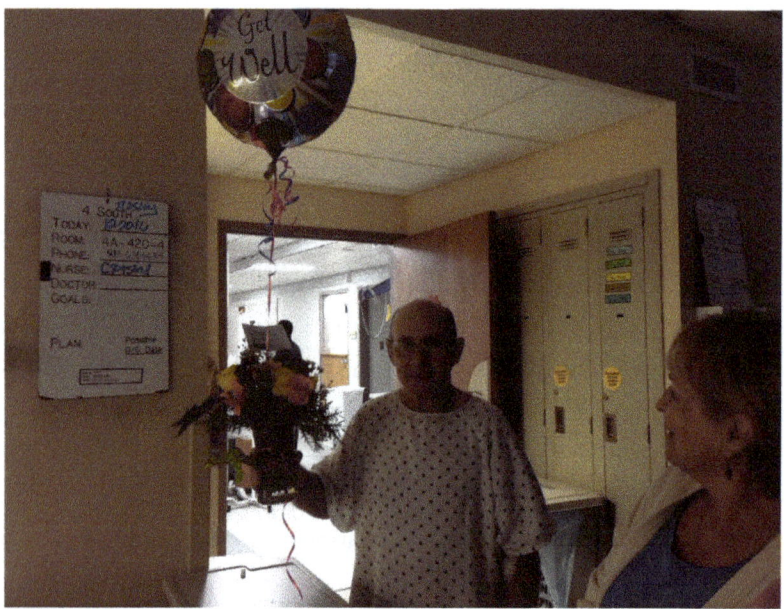

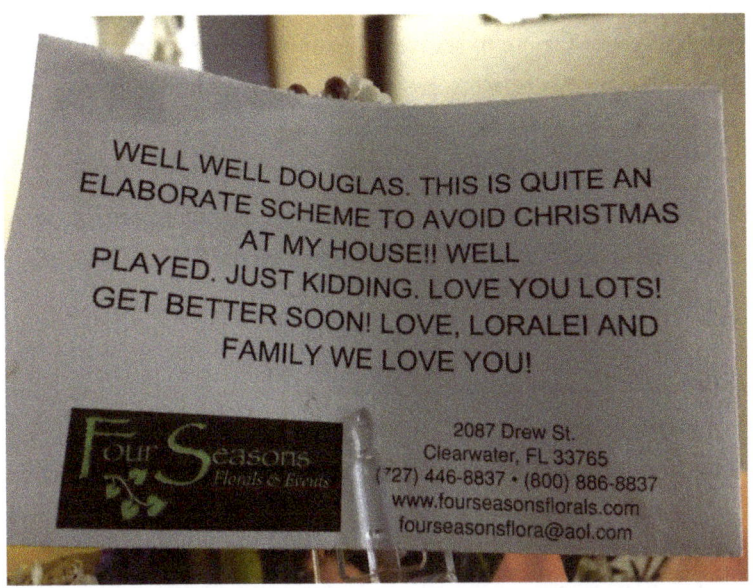

DECEMBER 29, 2016

AM. The surgeon briefed us on what the surgery might or might not entail. She said the plan was to perform a Whipple Procedure. This would remove the mass and areas that were affected by the mass. This procedure is an extremely long one. Once in there, the mass would be biopsied to determine the exact nature of the mass. I was pretty sure they already knew what we were up against. She also said there was a good possibility that the mass was already extensively integrated with the blood system to the point that removal might not be possible. That would mean that the mass was nonselectable.

PM. The surgery was not the long one we had hoped for.

"This will kill him."

JANUARY 1, 2017

I drove back home to my cabin. I opened my planner to January 1 and on it I had written, Apply to Peace Corps. This was not the time. Doug would be my Peace Corps. He was recovering from his surgery which had included a bypass so that he would be able to eat and drink again. The prognosis was that the bypass would take about three to six weeks to start functioning. While Doug had been told of his diagnosis, we were not certain that he really comprehended what he was being told. He was under a lot of pain medication and very sick. I called him daily. He was on 4 South and had some other patients in the ward with him. Shelley was a jewel, visiting him daily. My daughter Loralei and her family had rushed down to see him but had to go back home for work and the kids' school.

JANUARY 5, 2017

Doug was still throwing up. A storm was coming to my cabin in Blue Ridge and I ended up snowed in that weekend. A feeding tube called a GJ Tube had been put into Doug's abdomen so he could receive liquid nourishment until he was able to eat and drink again. There was a bag attached to the tube that collected gastric output that was unable to flow into his small intestine due to the mass. He also had to record the gastric output on a log. He was taught to calibrate the machine that pumped his formula into him. This output monitoring would let us know if there were some issues. We were told that as his bypass became functional, the gastric output would decrease. Once it had decreased to the point that this tube was no longer necessary, the apparatus would be removed. He would then get rid of the bag and begin to eat normally again.

JANUARY 11, 2017

Doug was sent home to Shelley's.

JANUARY 15

Doug was back in the hospital. We had been hoping he would eventually get well enough with the bypass to go to his home, eat and drink once again, almost like normal. Things just did not look good. I called him every day, sometimes twice a day. I felt so guilty that I was not there. We were given a code that we used to access his nurses and doctors. They said sometimes it took a while for the bypass to function completely. I would ask him what his gastric output was—I was almost obsessive about the numbers.

I realized I needed to pack up my cat and move to Florida to be with Doug. I was hoping that perhaps he could come and live with me once he stabilized and did not need constant care from the VA. I contacted a home security service to come to install a camera and an alarm system. I also struggled to decide how to best keep my cabin functional while I was gone, not knowing how long I would be gone or how often I would be able to return.

I belonged to a group of women called the Blue Jays, short for Blue Ridge and Ellijay. You had to be a single woman and live in the area of Blue Ridge and Ellijay. As I reached out and talked about my brother's diagnosis, many offered to help. Three of them, Sue Hoagland, Carrie Cirrito, and Marcia Lehman agreed to become cabin checkers for me while I was gone. Once a week one of them would go to my cabin, water my plants, check the HVAC, plumbing, and crawl space. What a gift they gave me! I will be forever grateful for the peace of mind that they provided. A security system and camera are good, but when someone physically checks your home out it takes so much pressure off of you. I also had some neighbors, Bruce and Denise Burns, who parked one of their vehicles in my driveway for months to give the appearance that someone was there fulltime. During the winter months when there is low occupancy in my cabin community, there are break-ins in cabins that are second homes. We also often have power outages due to storms that can lead to frozen pipes.

On **February 7**, with a new laptop for my computer work, mail forwarding, and the security system installed, I put my cat Ninja into his pet taxi, packed a bag with eight changes of clothes and headed to Tampa. February 8 we were scheduled to meet with Doug's surgeon and the oncologist.

FEBRUARY 8

We met with the surgeon and then with our oncologist, Dr. Samantha Shams. She was very pretty, extremely knowledgeable, and honest without being brutal. My oldest daughter, Liberty, who is an equine surgeon, was part of the conference via cell phone. She asked many questions that the rest of us had no idea to ask. It was at this meeting with Dr. Shams that I think Doug finally understood that he was going to die. He began to cry and Shelley with him. I was a frozen zombie from the abyss. I had prepared a list of questions and had my pen out as Dr. Shams answered each one. Her compassion was evident and we felt it.

"I cannot save you, Mr. Miller, but I can give you some time."

Time, I thought. Time for a possible breakthrough cure? Time for us to be able to cling to him and make the time count. Time to let him know how much he means to us. Time for me to still have my best friend.

I had wild thoughts of us traveling the world. Seeing whatever he wanted to see. But first he had to heal from his surgery and get back to eating and drinking. He had already lost over 30 pounds.

Dr. Shams, whom everyone called Dr. Sam, offered two courses of treatment. One was to sign up for a clinical trial and the other was the standard chemo treatment for Doug's type of pancreatic cancer. Doug chose the standard chemo route, saying he did not want to be a guinea pig. So Dr. Sam outlined a chemo regime that would begin on February 23. This was the earliest they could safely start following his surgery. It would also allow time for the bypass to start to work so he could eat and drink. At the present time he was still on the feeding tube.

He was hooked up to the machine that pumped the formula into his small intestine from 5 p.m. until 7 a.m. The rate of the flow had to be slow enough for his body to accommodate it and utilize the formula. Doug had become a pro on how to program the machine. My sister and I learned how to drain the bag that was attached to his abdomen as well as how to administer the nightly feedings. We had to log the G-tube output and bring it to appointments.

Doug really hated the bag that was attached to him. He focused upon getting rid of it once the bypass kicked in enough for it to be removed. I think that he pushed the fact that he was going to die into the background as the bag became an obsession. The surgeon said that this should happen between three and six weeks post surgery.

My sister Shelley is the emotional one of the family while Doug and I are more like Spock of Star Trek. After we left the gut-wrenching meeting with

Dr. Sam and returned to my sister's, she loaded us up on the Gator and drove to the back of the property. She had decked the Gator out in helium balloons. She made us get out and told us to start punching the balloons while she held them. I looked at Doug uncertainly and he gave me a similar puzzled look.

Shelley said, "When you get bad news you need to find a way to let it out, to release the horrible feelings so I will hold the balloons while the two of you hit them." She was crying and everything. It was awful. I felt somewhat stupid and overwhelmed at the same time, but I kind of slapped at them so she would feel better. Doug just stood there.

Shelley was relentless, "Hit them, Doug! Hit them now! Hit them with everything you've got!"

Well, he did. But his hand sideswiped one of the balloons and his fist connected with her hand hard enough to leave a bruise and her hand hit her face. Oh hell, I thought. This is very weird.

So, there we were, my sister's hand with a bruise and my poor brother looking so dejected that I decided the best thing to do was laugh. And that actually helped all three of us. You can go through life laughing or crying. Right now we were going to laugh.

265-29-3117

Site of the Feeding Tube

There are many area of the body that the tube feeding can be given. All of these areas use the feeding as if it were a regular meal.

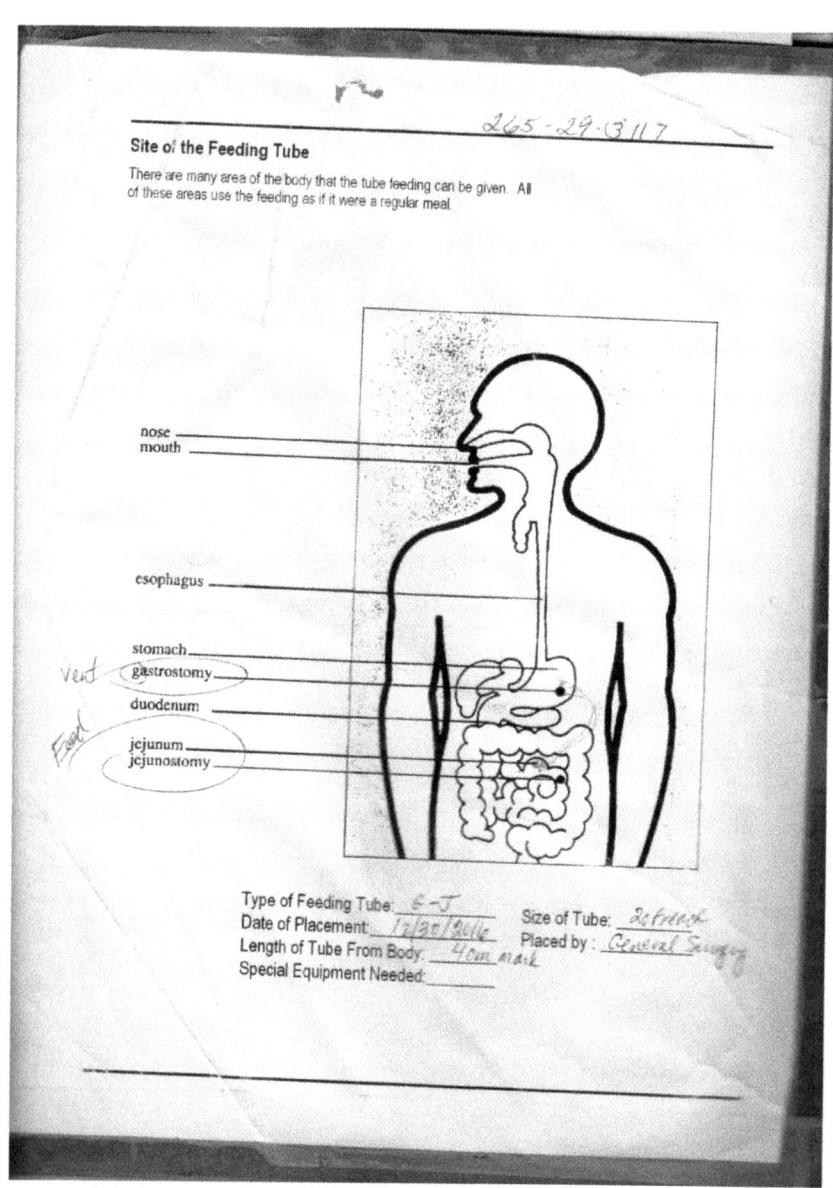

- nose
- mouth
- esophagus
- stomach
- Vent — gastrostomy
- duodenum
- Food — jejunum
- jejunostomy

Type of Feeding Tube: G-J   Size of Tube: 20 French
Date of Placement: 12/30/2016   Placed by: General Surgery
Length of Tube From Body: 4cm mark
Special Equipment Needed:

Bring to follow up appt.

G-Tube Output

Date	Time/Amount	Time/Amount	Time/Amount	Time/Amount	Total for Day
1-12-17	8:30am 1,600ml				
1-13-17	8:00 2,000				
1/24/17	vomit 800ml				
1/25/17	8:45 1100	11:00 200	7:15 300	11:00pm 500	2100 mLs
1/26/17	11:30 900	3:35 650	11:06 1100		2650
1/27/17	7:45 910	11:00 425	4:00 375	10:00/R 800	2510
1/28/17	7:35 1070	11:00 450	3:45 700	10:00 390	2630
1/29/17	8:00 1150	11:00 350	3:40 400	4:30 575	2475
1/30/17	7:00 1000	11:00 450	4:00 325	10:30 500	2275
1/31/17	7:30 1000	11:00 200	5:00 300	10:00 400	1900
2/1/17	9:50 700	11:15 640	4:00 410	9:40 700	2490
2/2/17	7:15 950	11:00 300	3:45 400	4:45 400	2050
2/3/17	7:15 1100	11:00 200	3:50 260	10:11 700	2250
2/4/17	8:00 1700	11:30 250	4:00 350	10:00 700	2600
2/5/17	9:00 1350	12:30 200	4:00 250	10:20 9:50	2750
2/6/17	8:30 1900	12:35 400	3:45 250	9:30 3:00	2850
2/7/17	7:10 1300	11:00 500	3:00 300	9:30 900	3000
2/8/17	7:20 1600	11:30 790	4:15 500	10:00 900	3790
2/9/17	7:40 1820	11:30 700	4:00 9:50	10:00 990	4060
2/10/17	8:00 1690	12:00 500	4:15 420	10:00 900	3510
2/11/17	8:15 1500	2:00 250	4:00 300	9:50 750	2800
2/12/17	7:50 1400	12:00 400	4:00 325	10:0 800	2930
2/13/17	11:00 1400	12:00 850	4:00 800	10:00 1200	4250
2/14/17	7:30 1800	11:50 680	4:05 1000	10:00 1050	4520
2/15/17	7:10 1650	11:40 725	2:30 480	7:50 1250+400	4505 ER
2/22/17	4:00 250	9:45 900			1150
2/23/17	5:30 1750	2:25 1050	4:30 500	10:00 700	3630
2/24/17	8:00 1000	11:30 1010	4:00 1200	10:10 1350	4560
2/25/17	7:00 2300	12:00 1000	4:00 1050	10:00 1100	4450

Miller Instructions   *Leave Gtube portion to gravity all the time*   1/24/2017

(handwritten: 8 AM)

6am: Disconnect Tube feeds and flush J TUBE with 20ml of water then:
- Erythromycin 250mg crushed mixed with water and put down jtube
- Metoclopramide 10ml in J tube (flush with 20-30 ml water after)
- Refeed g-tube output via pump at 500ml/hr with max of 1000ml. RECORD how much output in bag every time you do this to bring to follow up.

8am: *(handwritten: Salt tab)*
- Levothyroxine 0.075mg – crush and put down j tube
- Aspirin 81mg-chewable
- Lansoprazole 30mg (under the tongue)

11am: Refeed g-tube output via pump at 500ml/hr with max of 1000ml. RECORD how much output in bag every time you do this to bring to follow up.

12pm:
- Metoclopramide 10ml in J tube (flush with **250 ml** water after)

2pm: *(handwritten check mark)*
- Erythromycin 250mg crushed and put down jtube mixed with water, flush with 20ml water after

---

4pm:
- Refeed g-tube output via pump at 500ml/hr with max of 1000ml. RECORD how much output in bag every time you do this to bring to follow up.

6pm: *(handwritten: 5:30, Salt tab)*
- Metoclopramide 10ml in J tube (flush with 20-30 ml water after)
- Restart tube feeds at 100ml/hour *(handwritten: 250ml flush every 4 hours — 750ml only in bag)*

8pm: *(handwritten: 02:00)* pause tube feeds and take then restart feeds.
- Erythromycin 250mg crushed and put down jtube mixed with water

---

(handwritten: 10:00) **12am**: pause tube feeds and take then restart feeds.
- Metoclopramide 10ml in J tube (flush with 20-30 ml water after)
- Restart tube feeds at 100ml/hour

- Nauseated? - Take ondansetron tab.
- Pain? – Acetaminophen/Codeine 15ml into J tube – flush before and after. Can take every 4 hours
- Constipated? Senna 5ml syrup via j tube, rectal suppository if no BM 12 hours after senna
- Keep journal with output and any issues.

Tube Feeding and Flush Orders

[handwritten margin notes: "updated 1/30/17"; column of numbers: 700, 400, 1160, 625, 125, 650, 1100, 132, ...]

Your Tube Feeding Orders

Every person is different and their medical condition[s] require certain tube feeding formulas. Your medical team has put together this feeding formula and plan specifically for you.

Formula name _Isosource 1.5 (5 boxes/day) (-50 mL, 8.45 oz)_

Set the pump at a rate of __100__ mL./hour for __12__ hours.

From __6:5__ AM/~~PM~~ through __6 7:30__ ~~AM~~/PM.

OR _Start with 2 cans (last 5 hrs) rinse bag when formula runs ~~out bag,~~ then add 3 cans and run until finish (another 7.5 hrs)_

Set the pump at a rate of _____ mL./hour.

Give _____ mL of formula _____ times a day.

OR

Give _____ mL of formula via feeding bag or syringe _____ times a day.

Your Flush Orders

by pump Flush your feeding tube with __250__ mL of water/saline __5__ times a day. _Add ~~water~~ to flush bag and set flush interval to every 3 hrs. If water left in bag when feeding complete do manual flush until water_
by syringe Do a __20__ mL flush before your feeding and a __250__ mL flush after your _is gone from bag._
feeding. ~~Give 250 ml c syringe at 4+8 Noon~~ Discontinue
(apprx)
Additional water flushes of _____ mL should be done _____ times a day when the weather is extremely hot and humid or if you have been vomiting or have diarrhea.

You will also need to do a __30__ mL flush after giving your medications each time _by tube._

So here we were. We were all living with my sister and her husband, Ron. There were three bedrooms and two bathrooms. But it was crowded, especially in the middle of the night when everyone had to get up and use the bathroom. For Doug that meant that he had to stop his tube feeding and unhook from the machine. One bathroom was at the end of the hallway where the three bedrooms were. The other bathroom was adjacent to the living room which meant a journey through the kitchen, dining room, and living room. This created an additional anxiety among the four of us. I think we were all afraid that someone would hear us pee. For crying out loud…we were a mess.

We wondered how he contracted pancreatic cancer. Our parents had lived to the ages of 85 and 88. Cancer was not widely prevalent in our family history. There was some heart disease (late in life) but there were also two grandparents who had lived well into their nineties. Upon learning of my brother's diagnosis, one of my neighbors, who knew Doug had been in the Marines, asked me if I was aware of the contaminated wells at Camp Lejune between the 1950s and February 1985. I was not. I went and researched after Doug confirmed that he had been at Camp LeJeune for a year in the 1970s. Doug also said that the VA had been sending out information on the contamination.

The wells were contaminated with trichloroethylene (TCE), tetrachloroethylene (PCE), dichloroethylene (DCE), vinyl chloride, benzene, and other contaminants. At the time of Doug's diagnosis, the VA recognized eight diseases as having sufficient scientific and medical evidence for a presumption of connection. As of January 30, 2017, the diseases were adult leukemia, aplastic anemia, and other myelodysplastic syndromes, bladder cancer, kidney cancer, liver cancer, multiple myeloma, non-Hodgkin's lymphoma, and Parkinson's disease. Other diseases also covered for care by the VA included esophageal cancer, breast cancer, renal toxicity, female infertility, scleroderma, lung cancer, Hepatic steatosis, miscarriage, and neurobehavioral effects. Pancreatic cancer was not one of them. Its causes were not known.

We also considered the contacts with possible carcinogens that Doug may have experienced in addition to his time at Camp Lejeune. Upon leaving the Marines, Doug worked for a pest control service. The last 20 years, Doug had been working in a plant nursery using many pesticides. So who knows?

Life now had a new routine as we waited for his bypass to work. His hatred for the bag was profound and he was also embarrassed by it. He did not want people to see his bag. Even though it was not a bag for waste products he thought people assumed that it was. It was as if his impending death was not the big issue, it was the bag. I would see him pick it up and look at it. He had not been able to eat or drink since December. Everything he tried to eat or drink gave him nausea at best and vomiting at the worst. All nourishment and medications were administered via his GJ tube. I would visualize a lake, representing his stomach, with a dam, representing his tumor that was blocking the entrance to his intestines.

Shelley and I learned how to operate the feedings, the refeeding of the gastric juices, the administration of all medications, the correct logging of all of the data that needed to be kept daily, as well as observing any changes in Doug. Doug was also experiencing lower back pain. We later learned that this was consistent with the type of tumor he had. We kept notes daily on what his pain level was.

As he recovered from the surgery, we struggled to find a balance on his feeding and refeeds. He was at first very tired. However, we started to see some progress as his weight stabilized and we adjusted the flow rate of his feeds and were given new medications to counter his nausea and vomiting. The only issues he faced with his bowels and bladder were how the medications interacted with normal functions. Some medications would cause constipation, others diarrhea.

Our hope was once the bypass functioned and the bag and tube were removed, he could go home or perhaps come home with me to the mountains. We even discussed some of the places he wanted to see. He made a list: visit friends and family, train trip out west, Kathy's cabin, and go to different parks. A cruise to Alaska was the favorite pick.

My kids came and visited. He really lit up when they were there. Playing gin rummy was a favorite pastime and would become part of our daily routine.

My sister put me in "The Hippie Bedroom" which had been her daughter's. It was not "The Hippie Bedroom" when it was Sarah's. I did enjoy the décor.

Doug's room was filled with cards of well wishers. My Loralei got him a Sports Illustrated Swim Suit Calendar and a Man Can filled with man stuff. His room was comfy but also functioned like a hospital room. He even had a bed that came from the VA that was adjustable. This was good as he had to recline at an angle due to his overnight feeding procedures. Liberty got a white board and put our medication and hourly schedule on it.

The grandkids enjoyed watching the Sand Hill Cranes that came nearly every day to the property. Ron made sure that some feed was out there and they became a part of our daily life, a sight we always enjoyed. The grandkids were fun with their energy and goofiness. It was hard to be unhappy when they were around.

Then there was this thing going on about facial hair. Both Doug and my son Travis began to sport mustaches. It was really hilarious to look at the two of them together and listen to their banter about who had the best "stache." Ron already had some facial hair as well as my son-in-law Ross. I could not remember Doug ever having facial hair before now. How bizarre. He even asked me why didn't I grow my hair long again like when I was a teenager. So I started to let it grow.

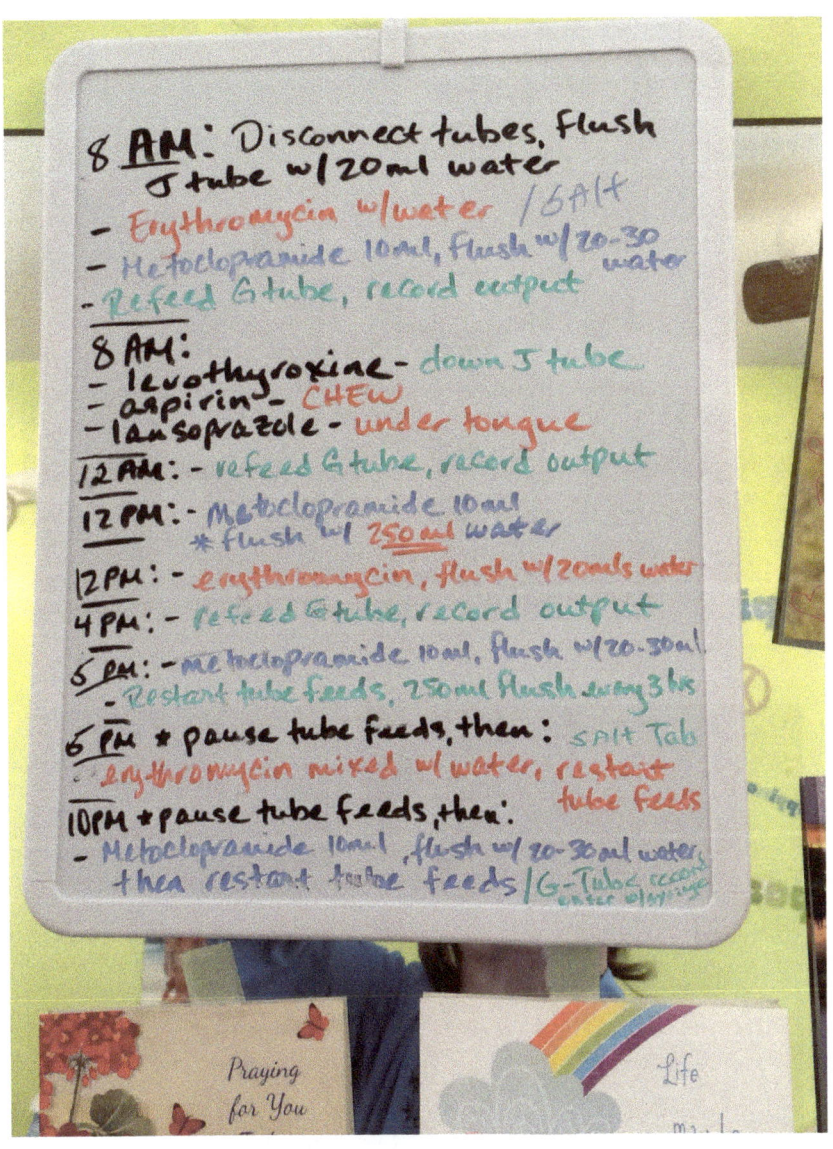

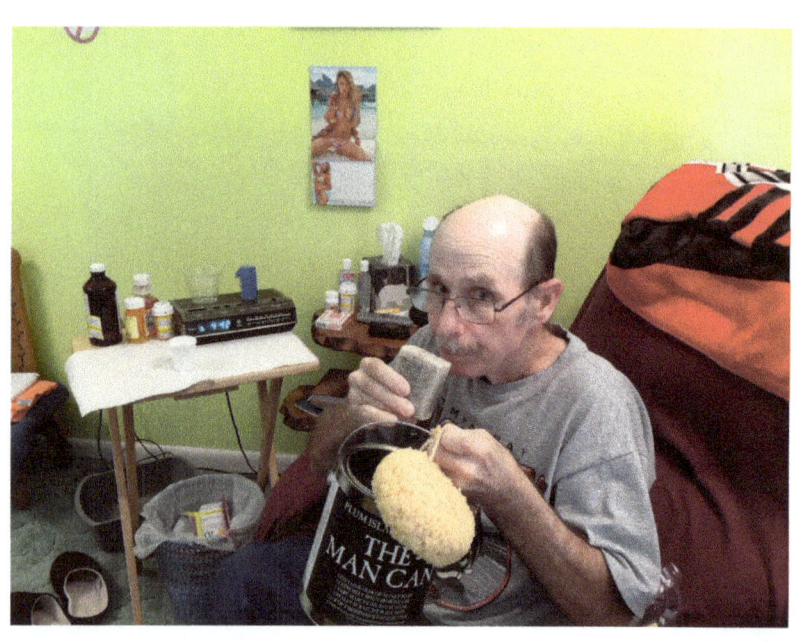

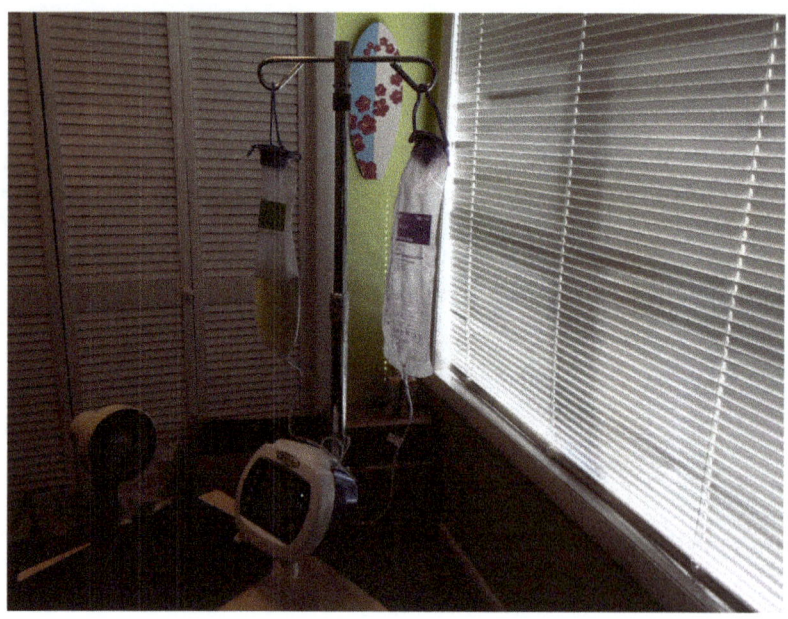

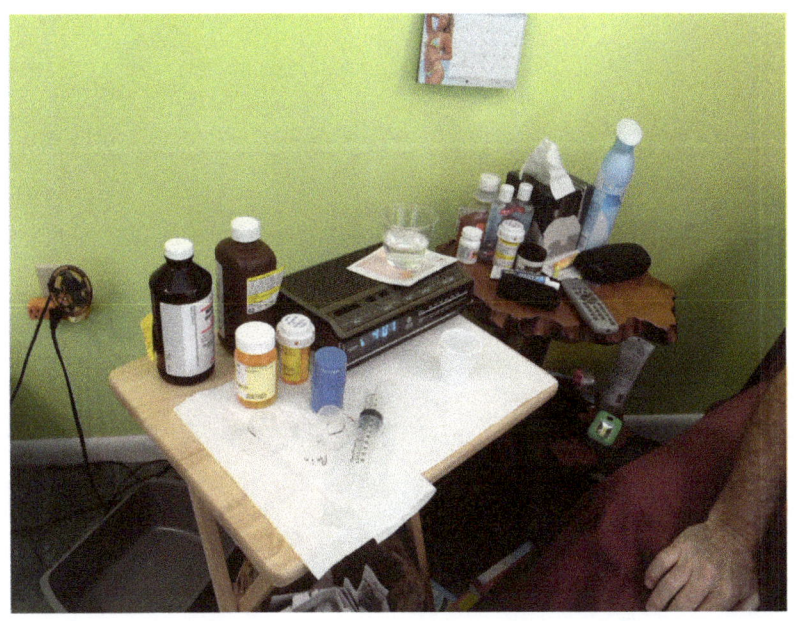

The drugs that Doug was going to be treated with were gemcitabine and abraxane. His first treatment was on February 23. Going for chemo means that there are strict protocols that must be followed. First we had to go to the hospital lab and have blood drawn. We then went to the chemo department where Doug's vitals were checked. If the blood work and vitals were okay, then we had to wait 2-3 hours for the pharmacy to mix his chemo. Once they were mixed and delivered to the chemo department, then he was hooked up and the drugs delivered intravenously. This took about two hours. This meant that chemo day was pretty much all that we did on that day. We normally reported to the lab for blood work at 7a.m.

Doug's chemo cycle was three weeks in a row, once a week, then one week off. After three cycles, a scan would be done to determine the progress of the therapy.

Parking at the VA was a challenge. This was February and many veterans will winter in Tampa to escape the colder weather elsewhere, so the hospital was really busy. There was a really great service that we learned to utilize—the valet service. We would pull up to the VA entrance and a valet would take our car somewhere to park it. Once we were finished, they would bring it right to us. I was really touched and impressed with how hard the valets worked. I wanted to tip them, but tipping was not allowed.

Chemo really wiped Doug out. For the four to five days after chemo, he spent more time in bed than anywhere else. By the time another chemo treatment came due, he was feeling better. Then back to bed again after. He was also having a lot of pain in his lower back. At first the pain medication was Tylenol codeine. We were recording pain levels daily. Towards the end of March, he was prescribed morphine.

When he first started on morphine, he would get loopy. The hospice nurse assured us that this was normal and that as he adjusted to the morphine he would get less loopy. Shelley and I joked with him that boy did he have it made. Free drugs and also his sisters were now his neighborhood drug dealers. The thing was he had some illogical idea that he needed to bear his pain instead of asking for relief for it. He was also afraid of becoming addicted. The hospice nurse came once a week and she always asked what his pain level was and he always lied. He said he was fine and he was not fine. This was something that I think he wanted to be brave about and not worry us. But you can't hide this kind of thing from two bossy older sisters. Especially when we all lived in the same house.

Doug was still unable to eat or drink. We did not let any visitors eat or drink in front of him. This meant that we also did not eat in front of him and Shelley did her best not to let the smells of cooking surround him. This was nearly impossible as his bedroom was directly across from the kitchen. I cannot fully communicate how this distressed us. Doug said he was not hungry and it did not bother him, but if he would lie about his pain then I did not believe him about the food thing. I developed a huge guilt complex about eating. It was like I needed to go somewhere and hide when I needed to eat or drink. Just think about how social eating and drinking are. Just think about how pleasurable eating and drinking are. I could not even take him on a scenic drive and stop somewhere and have a cup of coffee. I think that this bothered me more than any other aspect of his disease. As it turned out, my brother never, ever again in this last year of his life got to eat or drink anything.

THE BAG

All of our focus centered, for the time being, on getting rid of the gastric bag along with the attending tube feedings. We all wanted him to be able to eat and drink once again. This was entirely dependent on the success or failure of the bypass that had been done on his surgery December 29. As the days became weeks and then months, we were realizing that there was the strong possibility that Doug was never going to get rid of this bag. He hated the bag more than any part of his illness. I would see him look at it, see him look at the tube that went into his abdomen, and hear him say, "This is no way to live."

No it wasn't.

In March, after a scan to look at the functionality of the bypass, we received the news that he would in all likelihood die with this damn bag still part of his anatomy.

I think that this news was more devastating to Doug than his terminal diagnosis. He was so down. We all were down.

I would always try to make a positive or humorous comment to try and cheer us up. Sometimes I just kept it to myself.

"Good luck with that strategy, Kathy. Really? Oh yay! Doug you get to keep this top of the line medical equipment, free of charge from the VA. It comes in one size fits all and in colors that complement any style or fashion you desire. It fits nicely into a laptop carrier for your convenience. Easy to transport and hidden from view. An additional feature is the handy clip for you to hang on the side of your bed or chair. Replacement is done weekly or as needed by your friendly staff of Shelley, Ron, and Kathy."

I tried to imagine what it must feel like to have a tube sticking out of your abdomen with a bag attached. I even tried to hang some things from my blue jean belt hooks and then walk around to acquire some semblance of what he must be going through. But I knew that this was not anywhere near the reality of his situation. Such despair and hopelessness.

I decided that we would try a road trip to my cabin in Blue Ridge, Georgia. It was a straight shot up I-75 and would take between eight and a half to nine hours, depending upon the traffic in Atlanta. This meant that I would be the only one providing the nursing care for Doug. This thought was terrifying to me—that I would have the sole responsibility for my brother's life. No backup. Just me. After all, I was only a girl with a cat. I was not all that great or anything. Just a girl with a cat.

ROAD TRIP

On April 6, the day after chemo, with a non-chemo week ahead, Doug and I headed out. I was a nervous wreck, but it was the first opportunity get out and to do something with him, so I put my cat, Ninja, in the back seat in his pet taxi and put Doug in the front seat. As we started out, my sister's cat, Buddy, who had become great friends with Ninja, jumped upon the top of my car. It was as if to say, "Hey, where are you taking my friend?" I did not realize that he had tracked Ninja so closely.

I needed to make the trip as fast as possible since we were going to miss the noon refeed while on the road. We only made two stops. The first was in Valdosta for gas and a bathroom break. I also did get a Starbucks hot tea so I would stay alert. I felt guilty sipping in front of Doug. The next stop was at a rest area in Macon for a bathroom break.

I was surprised that Doug stayed awake the entire trip. Doug had always been one to nod off, even on short journeys. Also the chemo had been making him extremely fatigued and he had been spending more time lying down than up for several days after each treatment. Maybe he was terrified of my driving?

As soon as we arrived at my cabin, I got him situated in my bedroom. It has a breathtaking view of the Cohutta Mountains. I hooked him up for his feeding and he was soon fast asleep.

The next few days he was very fatigued. We had been logging his fatigue level and the day after our trip I logged it at a 10, the highest level. He did begin to be more alert and more interested in doing a few things as the week went on. We did not do a lot. I had a fire at night and we took a few scenic drives during the day and played gin rummy. We headed back to Tampa on April 13.

THE MOVE

After our return, Shelley took me aside and said that the week that we were gone made her realize that we really needed more space. We had originally thought that the living arrangements were only going to be needed for a few weeks. Now that we knew he would never get rid of his tubes and bag, the nursing that was required would only intensify when his condition worsened.

We were fortunate that there was a beautiful home in the back of Ron and Shelley's ten acres. It had been Ron's parents home until they passed. So it was made ready, internet and cable installed, and Doug and I moved in.

We fixed up a room for Doug that had a nice view of trees and field. Ron installed a bird feeder just outside Doug's window. It became a great source of joy, especially when the group of Sandhill Cranes became regulars!

My room was right down the hall from Doug with a bathroom for him just outside his doorway. My bedroom had its own bathroom adjacent to it. The kitchen and living area were separate enough for privacy and noise control. There was also another bedroom that was ideal for when my kids and grandkids came to visit. It also had a bathroom.

Shelley outdid herself in getting beds, linens, kitchen utensils, towels etc. She was a volunteer at a hospice store and made good use of the store for the items we needed. She also got a newer hospital bed for Doug. She was so very thoughtful and thorough that we lacked for nothing.

We began to develop a weekly schedule. We took turns with the nursing responsibilities and the feedings. On Sunday after the morning refeed, I was off until that evening, and the same on Mondays. We were trying to find a balance and avoid burnout. Ron also learned how to do all of the nursing, so we had enough of us to keep it all together.

I know that at times I became short and curt. I did lash out at Shelley for little or no reason. I hated what was going on. I think this is what they call anger displacement. I struggled on how to make the time good and meaningful for not only Doug but for all of us. How do you give joy in a joyless time? How do you penetrate the profound despair and depression that all of us shared? It was a struggle, not only daily, but hourly, minute by minute. I tried to be upbeat. I do not like to share sorrow and pain. I only want to share joy and happiness. I hate drama and emotional moments. There were times when the pain burst through. I would wake in the night and cry. One night Doug heard me and called out, "What is wrong?" I went into his room and held him and we cried together. Such anguish. Such despair. Such dread. Always the dread. And still today, April 29, 2020 in the middle of the corona pandemic as I write this memoir, that anguish reemerges.

I made a list of opportunities as I tried to sort it all out.

1. I had an opportunity to show my brother how much I loved him.
2. I had an opportunity to discover more about my brother.
3. I had the opportunity to be with my brother and care for him. I had

no responsibilities that would interfere and I was financially able to be with him. There was no job that interfered.
4. I had the opportunity to learn to value every second of life.
5. I had the opportunity to become the person that my brother thought I was, to become a better human being.
6. I had the opportunity to have a purpose, something to give my life meaning.
7. I had the opportunity to comfort my sister, Ron, and my children.

I knew that I was strong and that I could summon that strength and find a way to give love, joy, and laughter to not only Doug but all of us who were suffering.

TALES FROM THE VA

The Dammit Doll. One hospital visit, Doug was getting a scan. On a previous scan some technician, not a doctor, had made a note that Doug had a reaction to the chemicals involved but nothing was said to Doug, a doctor, or us. Dr. Sam saw this written in his records and went ballistic. She got on the phone trying to find out details about this supposed reaction, saying, "So now he has to have all these special procedures because some tech thought they saw something that they did not describe and did not inform?" She was not happy. Later I was in a store and came across a Dammit Doll. The only other time I had seen one was at my wedding shower and my mother gave me one saying, "Now that you have a husband you need to take this Dammit Doll as needed and whack it against something and say, dammit, dammit, dammit. It will help your marriage." So I bought Dr. Sam her own Dammit Doll, which she really enjoyed.

You look good. Every time we met with Dr. Sam she would remark, "Mr. Miller, you really look good today!" Doug would always reply, "You look good too!" And you know something? They both really meant it. I treasured their playful banter. It was so special. Doug really liked her.

Inhaled? We had some very interesting visits to the VA. Sometimes there were issues with Doug's tubes and we would have to go to the emergency room. On one occasion, as we waited, a man came in pushing an old soldier in a wheelchair. He loudly and proudly told everyone there that this was his father, a 100 year old WWII veteran who had been on the news as he celebrated his 100th birthday. He had also been featured in local newspapers. We were then advised that the reason for the visit to the ER was that his Dad, who only had three teeth left in his mouth, had gone to the dentist for some work and somehow during the procedure had either inhaled or swallowed part of a dental instrument. They were there to find out where this minute instrument part was located, either in his stomach or his lungs. The old soldier was also quite deaf and one of the reasons that his son was speaking so loudly. Well, a little while later Doug and I were in one of the units and right next to us we could hear the anesthesiologist loudly asking the old soldier, "I need for you to understand the risks of me putting you to sleep so we can remove your lost dental equipment. Our x-rays have located it in your stomach and we can still get to it now and safely remove it. Do you understand and agree?"

It was serious but also hilarious to Doug and me. For a time we were able to forget about our issue and try not to let anyone see us laughing. Evidently all went well for we never heard anything more about him.

Bladder Woman. When we would wait on chemo day for his chemo to be mixed, we often heard some bizarre stories. There was one woman who told me the same story about herself and a medical procedure involving her bladder while she waited for her husband to be treated. She told it to me more times than I care to remember, and always provided graphic details.

Doug would covertly tap me on the elbow if she was in the waiting room and whisper, "Your favorite person is here waiting for you, ha, ha, ha."

I would whisper back, "You better be nice to your drug dealing sister or I'll cut you off, ha, ha, ha."

Then we would both smile and say hello to "The Bladder Woman."

Hydrogen Peroxide. One of the chemo patients we encountered was "Bob the Hydrogen Peroxide Man." When his wife was out of hearing range, Bob divulged that he was pretty sure that his cancer was caused by his wife giving him hydrogen peroxide for the last 52 years. Doug and I just nodded sympathetically in agreement. Seems he still had the same wife and we wondered about that.

Ward Chatter. One night while Doug was hospitalized, we overheard the patient in the next bed have a rather confrontational discussion with the nurse.

"Sir, I am here to take your blood pressure."

"No, Goddammit, you are not taking my blood pressure!"

"Sir, we need to know how you are doing by checking your vital signs."

"I hate coming in here. It is like jail except you can't bail out. I am going to call the cops on you! You never let me get any sleep either."

"Sir, you know that you don't get any sleep in a hospital."

Bruhaha!

An Interview. One afternoon after Doug and I had been playing gin rummy, I told him that I wanted to write a book about him. I asked if that would be ok. He laughed and said ok, but that he was not telling me everything! Ha!

"What was your earliest memory?" "Going across the country to Florida and we stopped and picnicked."

"That was when we had that large picnic basket wasn't it? I remember that we had a small cook stove, and Dad had taught me how to light the sterno, and he would cook us hamburgers. There weren't any fast foods like there are today."

"I also remember when we were camping out on Honeymoon Island and you broke a piece of firewood that cut into your eye. We were stuck there until the tide came back in."

"I also have a bad memory of when I got caught stealing a candy bar. I was going to have to go to Juvy Court. The worst thing was that Dad was off on a trip and Mom said, "Just wait until your father gets home!" There was a song out then, 'See you in September.' I was sure that I was going to Juvy Jail and would not be out until September."

"When was your first kiss?"

"I was 15 or 16. We had moved to Maine after Mom and Dad got divorced. Her name was Vicky Churchill. My best friend in High School was Bob Quarry. You could not get in trouble in Washburn, Maine...everybody knew your business. I got in trouble when I set off some fireworks and had to go to Juvy Court in Caribou. Another time I went to get some beer for my friends and myself. The local cop pulled me over and took the beer. I had a hard time explaining that to my friends. I know good and well that cop drank our beer."

"How about girlfriends"?

"I was pretty serious about a girl who was in the Navy when I was stationed in the Philippines. She was from Pennsylvania. But we both shipped out to different places."

"Why don't you want to read books anymore? You always had a book going and now you don't read them anymore."

"I don't know. I just don't. It's hard to get into a book anymore."

"What was your worst fear?"

"When I had to rappel off a 70-foot cliff while in the Marines. No wait...it was when that doctor told me that I had one year to live."

"What do you think happens when we die?"

"I think it is like going to sleep."

"Do you believe in God?"

"Sometimes. I just don't know. I am not much on all that religious stuff. Guess I am going to find out."

"Well, when you find out will you let me know if you can?"

"Sure."

"Just don't do any haunting or stuff like that, okay?"

"Maybe I'll just pull your hair like I like to do."

"So, if I feel my hair being pulled and no one is there, that is you?"

"Probably. Ha, ha, ha!"

"Bruhahaha!"

IN THE NIGHT

I awake. Sometimes at 2 a.m., sometimes at 4 a.m., 3:30 a.m. I often will hear him crushing the pills for the morning medications or the plink as he puts some of them in a small amount of water to dissolve. The machine that pumps his feeding is functioning. I hear it sigh and whoosh. All is well. He lives still.

I go and look in on him. It is like being a new mother all over again. He is so tired. He sleeps. The light from the night light glows. His face is a death mask. My little brother. I gently kiss him on his forehead and go back to my room to sleep.

I once changed his diapers. Mother believed in teaching us all to do everything. Doug is six years younger than I. I used to plunge his diapers in the toilet before putting them in the damper.

Now we are getting old. I am 67. He is 61. He has stage four pancreatic cancer. He will die. Four months to a year is all he has left. How do I make moments of joy for him?

I always thought that Doug and I would end up living together in our old age. But not like this. He was supposed to live at my cabin while I went off to the Peace Corps. My version of saving the world. A dream since I was 18. Now I am trying to save my brother, as best I can. I will not be good enough. He will die. Doug will never eat again. Doug will never drink again. Yet he is condemned to live.

There is no God. Total bullshit. Suck it up, Buttercup. Death…the final frontier.

I am awakened in the night. I hear him down the hall. I hear him breathe. I hear him hook back up to the machine. I hear the pump start back up. All is well. I go back to sleep.

Such a simple man. Such a good man. Such an inspiration.

This house feels like a tomb.

Doug is so grateful. I do not deserve his gratitude. There are times I hate my life. There are times I hate myself. There are times I am so selfish and self centered. I am not the person he thinks I am. I will have to work on becoming the person my brother believes me to be.

MAY 2017

On May 6, Shelley and I went to an AARP Caregivers session. It was interesting to listen to other people as they shared their experiences. Some were long-term caregivers who had either patients or loved ones who were suffering from conditions that lasted for years. We were the only ones there with a terminal patient. We learned about taking care of ourselves and how important it was. Care giving is draining.

Doug had been reluctant to go out in public because of his gastric bag. Most people assumed it was some kind of fecal or urine bag. He was embarrassed about it. So Shelley found a laptop case at the hospice store and it was perfect for storing his bag. She was always so good at figuring out ways to make everything better. It had a shoulder strap and unless you really looked with great detail you would not see the tube that came out from his t-shirt and into the bag.

Now that we had that issue solved, we worked on getting him to go out and do a few things. Shelley arranged for a private tour of Big Cat Rescue. Yes, this was the same Big Cat Rescue featured in Netflix's Tiger King. Big Cat Rescue was only a mile or so from where we all lived and Ron had done water servicing for them. They put us in a golf cart and gave us the royal treatment. We really appreciated this kind and generous gesture.

Next I was finally able to convince him to go to the movies. Before he became sick, Doug and Shelley went to the movies regularly. May 9 we went and saw *Guardians of the Galaxy*. There were some awkward moments when we went in since they had to check his bag carrier. I hated to see how this humiliated Doug. The man who let us in was very nice and once we started going on a regular basis would just motion us on in. I had to schedule movies between feedings and refeeds. We usually went to the early morning or early afternoon matinees.

May 10. I took Doug on a scenic drive over the Sunshine Skyway. It was a really pretty day and he seemed to enjoy it. We would also drive over to his home every few days and check on things. One of the best parts of the drive was seeing the Osprey and Eagle nests.

May 11 I took Doug to the Lowery Park Zoo. He was strong enough to be out walking for around an hour and a half. These trips took place the week that he did not have chemo. The weeks that he had chemo, we would only have one good day of the week to do anything. He would be too fatigued from the treatment.

May 12 Loralei came down. Doug just loved it when the kids came. We took a scenic drive to Tarpon Springs and Honeymoon Island. While she was there, Loralei and I went to the movies and dinner for Mother's Day. The movie stopped during the showing as it had technical difficulties. I never did see the rest of it.

I had gone ahead and purchased a year's pass for both Busch Gardens and The Lowery Park Zoo. I also bought Doug a year's pass to The Lowery Park Zoo. He told me that he did not want to go to Busch Gardens, but was fine with the smaller zoo. We usually went to Lowery Park first thing in the morning after he was done with refeeds and medications. We really only had one week out of four that we did much since the three weeks that he had chemo wiped him out. On May 17, we had an assessment with Dr. Sam. The spot on his lungs was gone, as was the one on his liver. However, his tumor was the same size and his CA19-9 numbers remained high, dropping from the 500s to the 400s. Zero to 35 is considered normal.

I had some doctor appointments as well as cabin maintenance that I needed to take care of, so we decided that I would go home to my cabin for 10 days in May. I scheduled everything I needed to handle for that time frame. I was torn about going. At times I wanted to get away, only to discover that I could not wait to get back to Doug. This conflict occurred even with just a quick trip to get a fast food dinner. I would only be gone around 15-20 minutes but experienced such heightened anxiety that I was almost sick to my stomach. I was looking forward to seeing my cabin which I had only bought two years before, but I had many a sleepless night before I left worrying about how Doug would do. I was also concerned about leaving Shelley and Ron with the total responsibility. I felt guilty about having any joy about going.

I left on May 20. I saw the dentist, the dermatologist, the AC/HVAC guy, and my family doctor. I also was able to help with the Friends of the Library Book Sale and participated in the Spring Arts in the Park Blue Ridge Poets and Authors book sale. I called Doug every day, sometimes more than once. I really missed him. I awoke every day with dread and guilt. I used to say to them, "Hey, let's go on a run my friends, Dread and Guilt." There were many moments of self hatred. I returned on May 30.

JUNE

I had scheduled a book event with my book, *Dear Dad*, at the Baldomero Lopez Veterans Home on June 2. Our mother had lived there towards the end of her life. As a VA facility, they were very cognizant of the military service that their patients shared and I was to talk about my Dad's letters and WWII experiences. Doug went with me. I was surprised that he wanted to go, but so very happy that he did. I was a nervous wreck as I do not like to get up in front of people and talk. There was one gentleman who spoke up during the presentation, "Yes. I was there. I knew him." He was perhaps a bit mistaken, but it was fine.

The next day I went to see *Wonder Woman* and for some reason Doug did not want to see it and stayed with Shelley. I never really found out why he did not want to see it. He loved all of the Avenger movies and it is a mystery to me.

June 7 Doug and I went to see *Pirates of the Caribbean*. Later that afternoon, the nurse came and trained Shelley and me on the correct administration of fentanyl patches. He was started on a low level one. The patches were put on his back below his shoulders where there was some muscling. We had to alternate the patches and they were changed every three days. He was still getting morphine as well. The patches did make a difference. At first, as his body adapted to them, he was a little loopy. But it was a nice loopy. We continued to struggle to balance diarrhea, nausea, dry heaves, and pain levels. All of this was logged and it did help us mitigate all of the symptoms. He was weighed every week when the hospice nurse came.

I had been spending a lot of time on the internet researching pancreatic cancer and joined the Pancreatic Action Network. I would get emails and updates on the latest developments. In one email, the FDA had approved Keytruda for use. When I read that, I called Dr. Sam. She had his profile tested to see if he had the mutation that was favorable for Keytruda use. Unfortunately, he did not, so this was not a viable treatment for him. So depressing.

I had been recording Stephen Colbert and Doug enjoyed watching the opening dialogue. We also watched some of the Comey hearings.

June 9 We went to Lowery Park Zoo again. We had a favorite monkey that looked like a lion with his mane. He was small, orange, and very active. He was really very interesting and fun. For a time there was a dinosaur exhibit and the dinosaurs were animated, making the visit even more fun.

My cat Ninja had adjusted to the move very well. He would spend time with Doug, at times sleeping with him. Ninja had rarely slept with anyone other than me. I would joke with Doug that he was a bad influence and had encouraged my cat to "sleep around."

Doug had moved his own cat, Shera, to our new home. Shera was an evil cat. She was black, with some dark brown mixed in. Doug and Shera had previously lived for years in an apartment on the property so she was well acquainted with the area. During this time there had been an active plant nursery that Doug managed. It had belonged to Ron's parents and once they passed, the nursery was phased out. Doug was still working there as the last of the plants were sold. Shera was so evil that there was a sign that said, "Do not pet the cat. The cat bites." You could pet Shera once and when you went to stroke her the second time, she would bite the crap out of you.

Well, our attempts to get Shera in the house with Doug did not turn out well, with one incident of Shera violently biting Doug! My sister had been taking care of Doug that day and she was a mess after it happened, crying and blaming herself. We were very cognizant that Doug's immune system was fragile as he underwent chemo and fought his cancer. Anyhow, Shera ended up living outside with plenty of shelter to choose from. Every morning Doug would walk down to the old apartment and work shed to feed her.

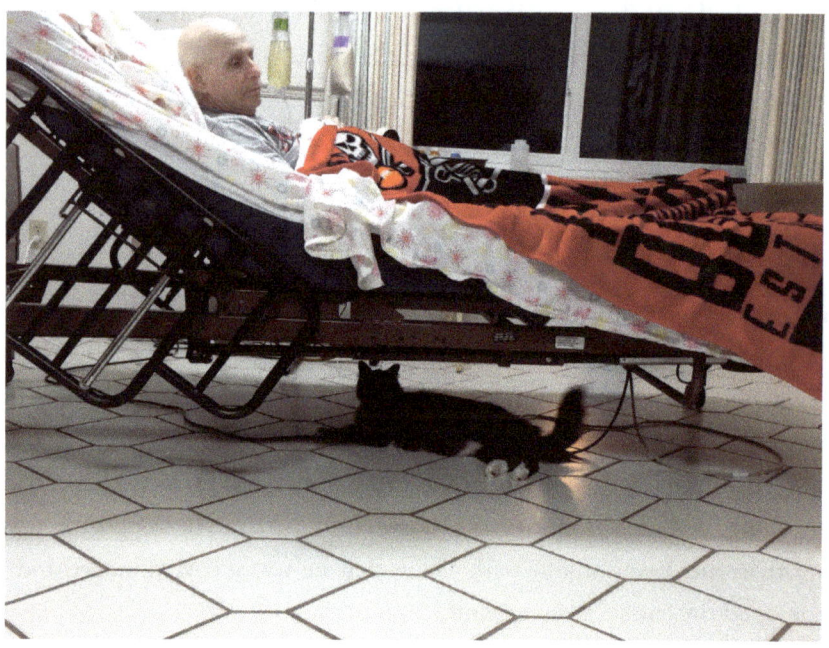

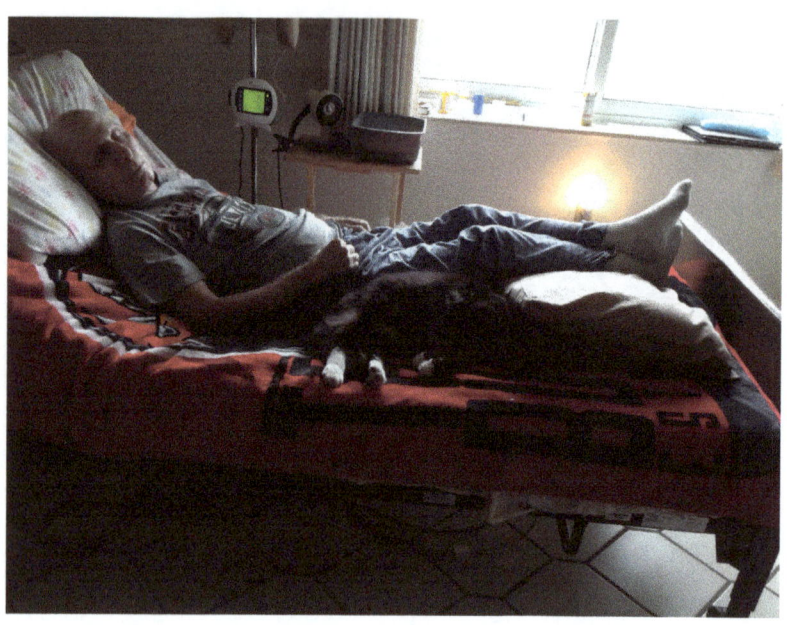

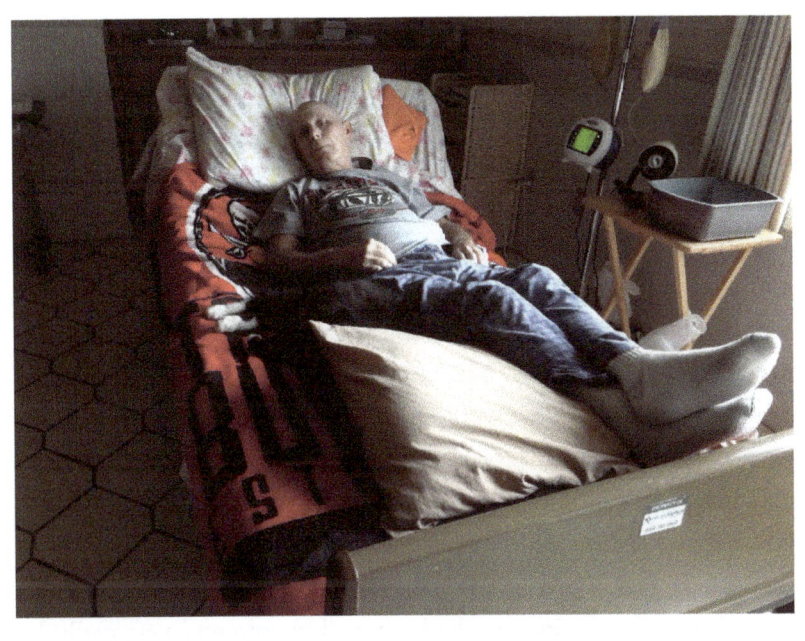

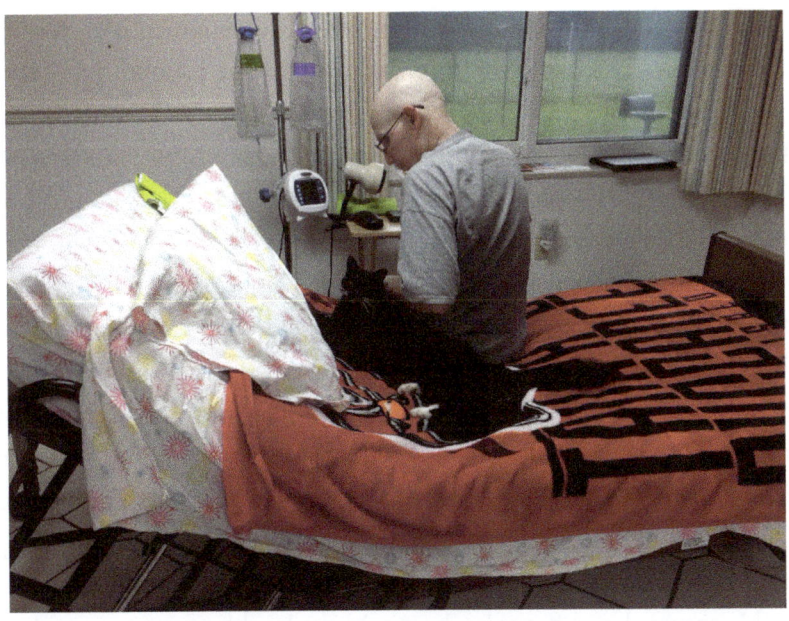

We went to see the *Mummy*. Almost weird considering our circumstances, but it was the kind of movie that Doug and I liked. We got a new hospice nurse, Zara, who ended up being the one who remained our nurse for the duration. She was so very kind. I wondered how she summoned the strength to do what she did. She was Muslim and wore very pretty head scarves. We thoroughly enjoyed having her and looked forward to her visits.

Liberty flew in from Tennessee for a few days and Doug just glowed! It was about this time that Doug decided to quit chemo. His days were spent nauseated and fatigued with only one day a week where he felt like doing anything. We were constantly juggling medications for nausea, for diarrhea, and for pain. He was on fentanyl as well as morphine.

There were times when we would have issues with the tube. We had to flush with water after every medication was given to get the medication to go into his small intestine. I used to try and joke that it was like gardening, only with a weird hose and Doug's abdomen as the garden.

Loralei and Travis were going to visit over the Fourth of July. Doug was becoming less fatigued since he had stopped chemo and was really looking forward to seeing them. Just before they were to come down, we had a major issue with his tube as it came partially out from his abdomen. We went to the VA ER and they reinserted the tube and inflated the balloon that held it in place. It came partially back out again and this time they did a stitch around it.

The kids were driving down and would arrive around 1 or 2 in the morning since they had left as soon as they had gotten off work. Well, around 1 a.m. I was awakened by Doug calling out to me. I rushed into his room. This time his tube had completely come out of his abdomen. I grabbed the tube and bag, put it into his barf bucket, placed a towel over his abdomen and we rushed to the VA. The kids arrived about 30 minutes after we had gone to the VA. I texted them and told them to just go to bed and I would fill them in on our status once I knew it. I did not wake Shelley and Ron up. For one thing, there was no time to lose, and why wake everyone up when there was nothing they could do?

Once there, we were told that Doug would have to be admitted. Replacing a GJ tube requires a specialized procedure involving scanning equipment. Since this occurred on a Saturday, he would not be able to get a new tube until

Monday, July 3. He was going to have to stay in the hospital during the kids' entire visit. He was really bummed out about that.

We did have one caveat. Doug requested his old hospital wing and got it. It was around 2:30 a.m. when we were brought to his room. As we approached the nurses' station, one nurse sought us out and greeted us, "Mr. Miller, you must have missed us. You couldn't stay away. It is good to see you again!" This was one of Doug's favorite people, Dakota. No matter the hour or circumstances, you could always count on Dakota to cheer you up. Doug then said with a grand flourish, "Mr. Miller, we have a grand suite for you with a splendid view! And you have this suite all to yourself!" Ha!

There was also some drama going on. There were two security officers engaged in a conversation with a patient. This patient was adamant that he was leaving and leaving right then and there. The officers were trying to explain that 2:30 a.m. is not a great time to check out and go wandering around. Brouhaha! We did get a kick out of that. Not a dull place, the VA. One nurse told us that they even had a patient call 911 on them. The patient told 911 that he had been kidnapped and was being held against his will!

The VA was a class act. We were treated with respect, compassion, humor, and integrity. I was touched by the dedication of the people who worked there. Not all veterans are very nice people and we often witnessed the workers bearing the brunt of insults and abuse by some patients. Their service was commendable. I don't know that I could do what they did day after day after day.

Shelley was not happy that I had not wakened her up at 1:00 a.m. I was trying to save her some worry, as well as sleep for her and Ron. Instead I ended up making her mad at me. Dammed if you do, dammed if you don't.

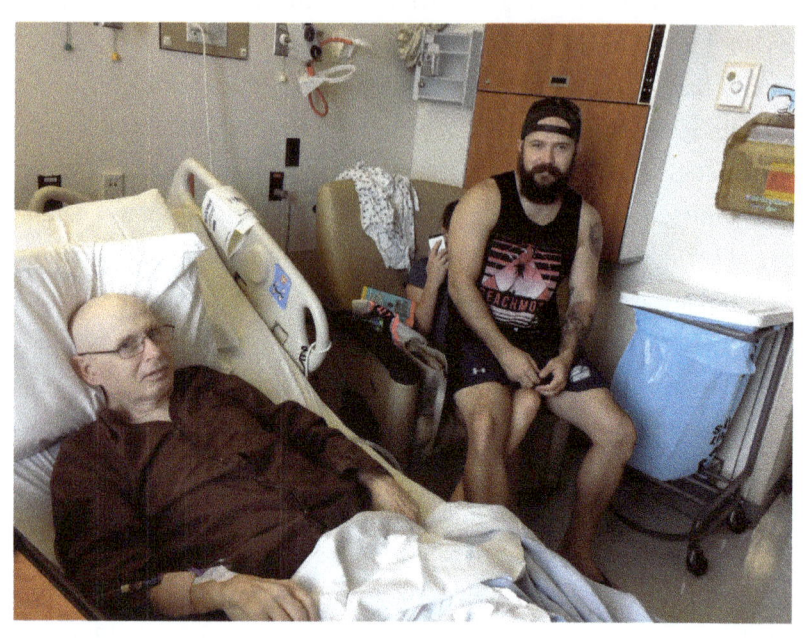

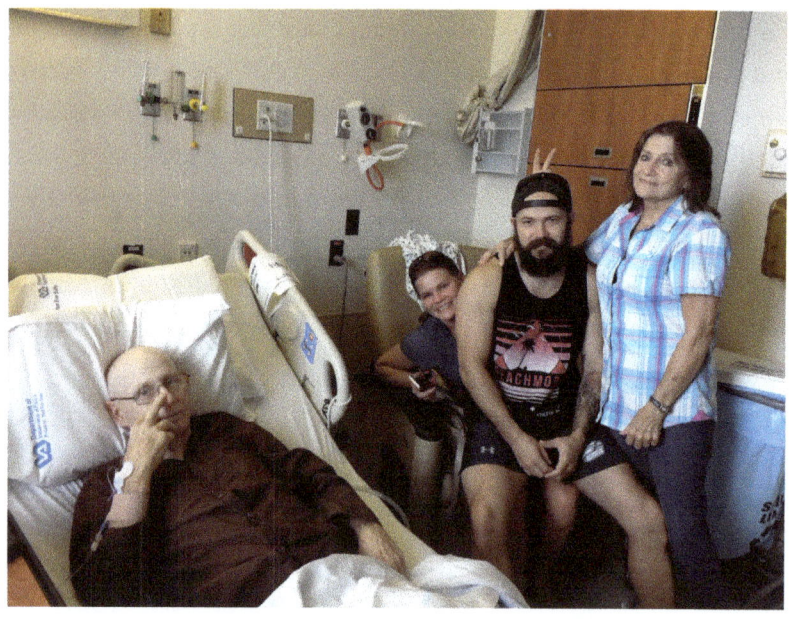

So Doug spent the holiday weekend that Travis and Loralei were here in the VA. The weekends are not the best time to need some extra "body work." But early Monday morning, they replaced his GJ tube and he went home.

We had some close friends come over for the Fourth of July. It seems this backyard fireworks by Ron and his friend were a yearly tradition. When I saw what was in the back of the truck, I was mildly terrified. There was some adult dimming of the senses and they proceeded to launch their pyrotechnic cache into the night sky. This was right up Doug's alley as he had a history with things that explode or burst into fire. As a child he had started a "campfire" in a closet, causing clothes to catch on fire and move into the attic. He was "somewhat involved" in a pasture fire, the truth of which is unknown to this day. As a teenager, he had been on the list of suspects setting off fireworks in the small town hamlet of Washburn, Maine.

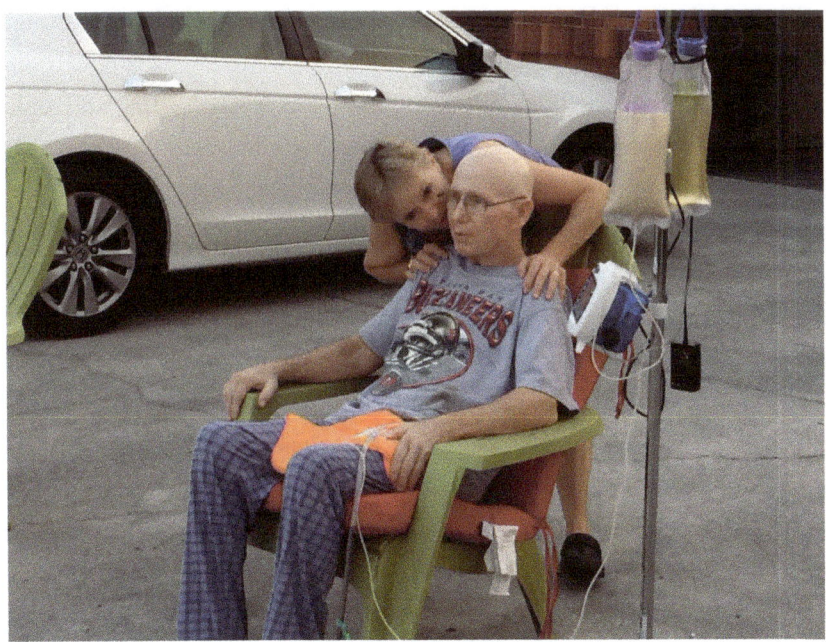

Doug was doing much better after stopping chemo. He was stronger and able to go out and about for longer periods of time. Every morning he would walk down to where his demon cat, Shera, was and feed her. He would then visit with Ron for a while before Ron would head out on a job. Ron had his own business of servicing water pumps and related issues.

Later in July, my 12-year-old grandson, Little Travis (not to be confused with my son Travis), came to visit. He arrived by plane and was pretty happy to fly alone. I took Little Travis to an all day trip to Busch Gardens while Doug hung out with Shelley and Ron. I had been in training for this event with my grandson since I would go every Monday, starting out on the roller coasters and finishing up with the animals. We had a blast and my legs held out better than his! As we were leaving, he was asking to stop and rest awhile on the way out! We were there for 9 hours and 40 minutes.

Another day, the three of us, Little Travis, Doug, and I went to see *War for the Planet of the Apes*. We kept up the pace by seeing *Dunkirk* and visiting the Sculpture Museum in St. Petersburg.

I also took Little Travis to a Tampa Bay Ray's baseball game at Tropicana Field. During the days he was there, he and Doug would play chess and we taught Little Travis how to play gin rummy. It was a really good time for all of us. For a moment or two, we were able to push away our thoughts of dying and despair.

Little Travis was no stranger to the devastation of cancer. He had lost his beloved Granny only a few years before to lung cancer. He brought a bright light into my life and Doug's with this visit. We hated to see him go home.

Towards the end of July, we began to have trouble getting the medications to go in his tube. We already had some experience with the tube becoming clogged, but this time it was different. One of the remedies that were recommended by word of mouth was to flush it with coke. This recommendation is not recommended in the literature that we had on hand. Well, we tried it any way and it did not improve the issue. We ended up going to the VA where a new tube was put in. After the procedure, we were told that there was a pinch in the tube and that it was a smaller circumference than the one before. The newest and latest was now functioning well.

We had begun two rituals. One was every night when I would kiss his forehead good night. I would say, "Semper Fi." He would reply, "Do or die."

The second one was in the morning. I would go in and say, "Good morning, how are you?" Doug would answer, "Woke up still not dead again today!" Thank you, Willie Nelson.

We now seemed to be on a plateau. Doug was the strongest he had been since his diagnosis. He made the comment that he wished he had quit chemo sooner. It is a no win choice. Live longer but sicker, or live shorter but better. Pre season football started and we had HBO where we watched the Tampa Bay Buccaneers on Hard Knocks. Doug was a season ticket holder and his home was done in Bucs Décor. Just a year before, my son Travis had given me two tickets to the Bucs Falcon preseason game in Atlanta. Doug had been visiting me that week and he really enjoyed the game, especially since the Bucs beat the Falcons (who are my team). I had to drive home two hours to the cabin after the game while he had an ill concealed smirk on his face! I would glance over at him and although he was not one to rub it in, his face was beaming happily! We would just laugh. It was good.

During this time, Doug and Shelley had been over at Doug's place watering the plants and checking on things. On the way back, Shelley stopped at the local Winn Dixie for some coffee creamer. Doug elected to remain in the car. As Shelley was leaving the store, she ran into Jameis Winston, the quarterback for the Bucs. She summoned the courage to ask if he would come over and say hi to Doug. She explained how much of a fan that Doug was and told Jameis of his condition. Jameis was gracious and very much the gentleman. He and Doug talked football. Jameis gave my brother more than the 15 minutes of football talk. He gave my brother a gift of realizing that there were many things that Doug could treasure in the time that he had left. Our family will forever be grateful for this kindness of this young man. He could have easily blown my sister off, but no. He showed compassion and thoughtfulness for a fellow human being. As I write this, I am sobbing with gratitude that a complete stranger was so good to my brother. Shit, I hate it when I cry. My eyes get all messed up and my nose is stuffed. Shit. It has been two and a half years and still I cry.

Well, Shelley really did one better. She got a card and we all signed it, thanking Jameis for his kindness. Shelley then dropped it off at the Bucs' office. She is really good at being thoughtful. Better than I am. Much better. She did not stop there either. She and Ron had a friend who was the uniform delivery man for Ron's business. This friend knew someone who worked in the Bucs' locker room. Doug's birthday was coming up and the friend was able to get Jameis to sign a jersey for Doug! Jameis made the comment that he was touched by receiving the thank you from us and was happy to once again do something for Doug.

We had some close friends, Donnie and Linda, come over to celebrate Doug's birthday. Donnie brought some Chinese Lanterns for us to light and send into the sky. It was serene, touching, and moving.

Loralei was so imaginative. She had a cake made from flowers sent to him!

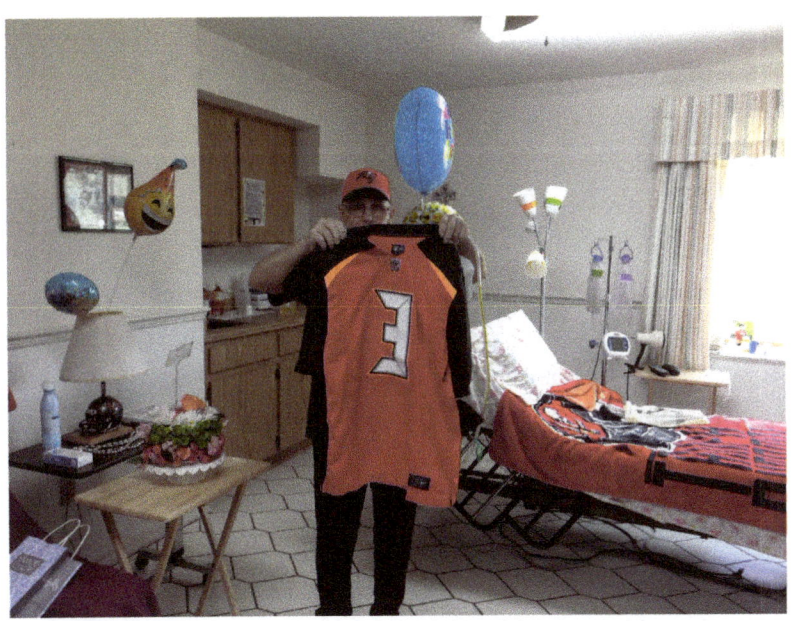

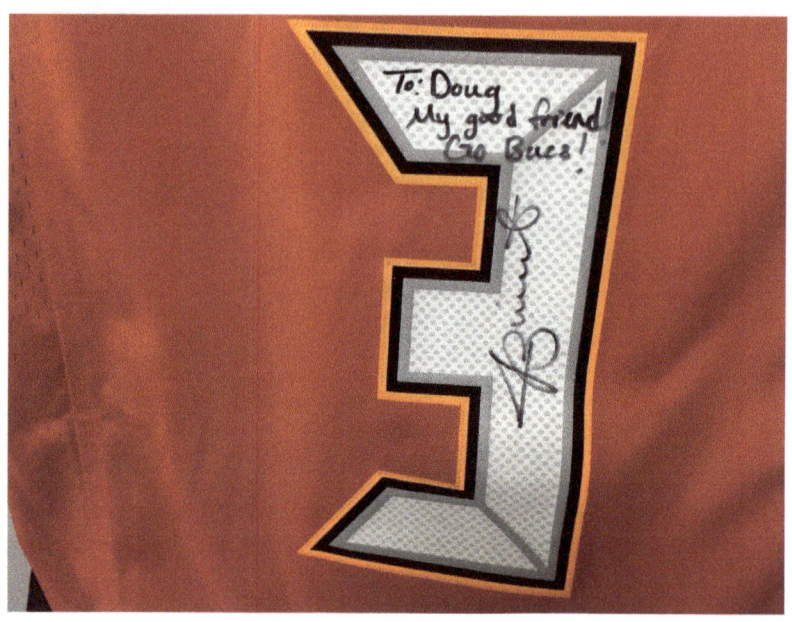

We started on a regular routine of movies, Colbert, football, scenic drives, gin rummy, Game of Thrones, the weekly hospice visits with our nurse, and visits from family and friends. There was laundry to do, a house to be cleaned, as well as the ordering of medications and supplies. When I was "off" Doug would spend the day with Shelley while I usually headed to Busch Gardens or any tourist site that was in the area. My kids came down often. They were so important, not only to Doug, but also for me. It is so draining to care for someone while they die. I do not really have the right words to convey how empty you become. An abyss opens up inside you that is filled with dread.

Every morning I would awake and tell my friend Dread, "Oh, hello. I see you are still here." Then I would go say good morning to Doug, get him medicated and his refeed going, and head out for my morning run (Shelley and Ron were just a phone call away, about 400 yards from their house to ours). That run was the glue that kept me together. That was when I did most of my crying. Nothing like a good crying run. After a run, no matter how long or short, I could handle anything. As I left for each run, my cat, Ninja, was usually inside. He would hang out with Doug and often slept with him. Sometimes he would sleep under Doug's bed.

My parting words usually were, "I will be back soon, but Ninja is here to guard you."

Doug would always reply, "I feel better already." Bruhahaha! My guard cat at his post watching out for my Marine Corp brother.

One evening after I had hooked him up for the night, there was a thunderstorm brewing. I went outside and lay on the concrete driveway. The concrete was warm and the air had begun to cool. Ninja lay down beside me. I thought to myself, 'God, if you even exist, make me a better person — never mind, I need to make myself a better person for my brother who lies dying. How can I be of help to him? How can I console him? How can I get him to live and not just exist?'

How astonishing that it is boring in some ways to watch my brother die. Each day has a monotony, a deeper surrender to inevitability. Doug has no idea what to do with the rest of his life. Would I? Is it up to Shelley and me to help him figure this out? Are we intruding? Should we let him alone? He is such a simple man. All has been taken from him — no food, no drink. No working with his plants, no gym. How does one remake the rest of their life? What is it that gives our lives meaning? Death perhaps. Without the deadline of Death, life would be without any value.

August 1 — Shelley and Ron are selling this place. Shelley sold her condo in Orlando that she had bought for her two girls to live in while in college there. Now they have found their dream home. It is on a lake about five miles from here. Today the realtor brought someone by to see the property which has the house that Doug and I live in, as well as the one Shelley and Ron are in. There is a shop and around 10 acres. Shelley sometimes seems very happy. She drives every week for a day and a night to babysit her grandchild in Orlando. I find that I resent her happiness. I am not a good sister. Now I must make sure the house is ready for the realtor to show at any given moment. I can't leave my bra hanging in the closet. This seems petty on my part to resent this. I was very mean to her. I am stressed and wondering if I will have to move us to Doug's place, which makes it more difficult to share care giving amongst us.

She said we would not have to move anytime soon. I guess that I felt she had no right to find any happiness while Doug was dying, which is not reasonable. But then emotional responses rarely are. I should have been happy for her and I was not. I hated myself. I considered moving us to my cabin. The problem is that he is comfortable with his doctors and the VA is only 20 minutes away. If we moved to my place, the closest VA is in Atlanta, about an hour and a half away. Then there is the issue of taking him away from Shelley, Ron, and his friends. If Doug did not have that hateful bag and tube, we could be so much freer.

In the middle of the night, I wake and want this whole thing to be over with. But the only way for this to be over with is for Doug to die. I do not want him to die. Dread. Stuck in the dying place. This place is a tomb.

I decided that Doug was doing well enough that we would go spend two weeks at my cabin. The tension between Shelley and I was pretty thick and time away would be good for everyone. They had sold the property and the closing was on August 21. For now, Doug and I would not have to move. It was cabin time. The solar eclipse would be viewable in Blue Ridge, so on August 20 we loaded up. I had Doug in the front seat beside me and Ninja in his pet taxi in the back. I made a list of what I needed for the duration, with some extra just in case.

Isosource 75	Two jugs	Barf Bucket
Bags 15	Water bottle	Kangaroo pump
Ceralyte 15	Ceralyte bottle	Night light
Gauze 15	All morphine	Table and lamp
Tape-spare roll	All Fentanyl	Thermometer
One box of gloves	All Metoclopromide	Big pillow
Salt tablets	White cups	Playing cards
Levothyroxine	Log book	
Two large syringes (for flushing)	Recording book	

Band aides	Med list
One G bag for backup	Kangaroo Cheat Sheet
Ethromycin powder	Amodium
Pill crusher	Coke

AT THE CABIN

We left Tampa around 8 a.m. and arrived at the cabin close to 5 p.m. I made the usual stops. Once again Doug stayed awake the whole time. He never drove again after he got sick.

Liberty, her husband, Ryan, and Travis and Ashli were at the cabin to greet us. Travis and Ashli's black Lab Leia was also there. Ninja did some impressive hissing to let Leia know just whose cabin it was. Ninja is not fond of dogs. It was so heartwarming to see them. Loralei was unable to come since she was sick and with Doug's condition everyone knew we had to keep him from contacting anything.

We put Doug in my room. I moved the bed to accommodate his needs. One thing that distressed me was the fact that he had to lie on his back and at an angle in order for the all night feeding to proceed according to plan. I was worried that since we did not have his hospital bed with its adjustable settings that there might be issues with the feed. Luckily everything worked fine. I set up his medications on the dresser. He had easy access to the bathroom. The cabin has a bath and a half. The half bath was next to his room. The bedroom I was in was on the other side of the half bath. If he needed me for anything, I was right there.

It was wonderful to be there. The sun sets on the side of the cabin where Doug had his view. So every night when he was hooked up and starting to sleep he could watch it set.

Ninja seemed happy to be home. He would sleep some with me and then some with Doug. What a great cat! Doug and I both liked to "complain" about how he took up too much room!

Due to work, Ryan had to leave the next morning, the day of the eclipse. Doug was so happy that he came, if even for a short visit. It was so considerate for him to drive three and a half hours each way just to put a glow on Doug's face. I will never forget how wonderful my children and their partners were to us. I am so grateful and their visits meant so much.

We did not have a total eclipse, but almost. Our favorite phenomena were the crescents on the stone walk entrance. We had our eclipse glasses and posed like celebrities. It was a really great day!

AUGUST 22

The kids left and headed to their respective jobs. Doug and I played some gin rummy. We would have some interesting conversations while we played rummy. Sometimes I would entertain him with Flash Foods war stories.

"Did I ever tell you about the guy who flashed his behind at me?"

"No, what happened?"

"I was pulling another midnight. My "sorry" third shift person called out at the last minute on a Friday night. She said something about her "Aunt Liddie" dying and she needed to be with her mother. The problem was I was pretty certain that she had buried "Aunt Liddie" about two months prior, another time that she unexpectedly had to take a weekend night off.

"So if anyone wanted to get some time off, they just told you that someone died?"

"Pretty much. It happened enough that I started to keep a log with dead relatives' names."

"Ha!

"Anyhow around 2:30 in the morning, a customer pulls up to the store and rang the bell on the night window. You remember me telling you about having a night window put in after we had a clerk shot and killed at one of our stores about a mile away?"

"Yeah. That was scary."

Well, this customer was unique. He had a dark shadow of a beard and was dressed in a black and white striped mini dress with a wide red belt. He sported red high heels, accessorized with a fetching red purse. Haphazardly perched upon his head was an ill fitting black wig that framed his very masculine features in such an endearing way that I immediately liked him, even if he was on the weird side. It sure beat the hell out of a guy in a mask carrying a gun.

"Was he a cross dresser?

"I am not sure. We were just down the road from Valdosta State University and sometimes if a student was pledging or just doing a dare they would come in at all hours in all kinds of outfits." I opened the night window. He asked for a pack of Marlboro Reds in a box. As he spoke he gave me big smile. I got his cigarettes and watched as he turned to leave. He gave me a big "shit eating grin" as he rotated a big, white, shiny, but extremely hairy behind in my direction!"

"Ha, ha ha! Did you call the police?"

"No. But I did call all of our other stores and entertained them with my story!"

"That is really funny."

Later I did some cabin chores, like pulling weeds. Then we went for a scenic drive to Tapoco Lodge in Robbinsville, Tennessee. The drive takes you through some spectacular vistas and it was a relaxing way to spend the day.

AUGUST 23

We took Ninja for his rabies shot in the morning. In the afternoon, Doug went with me to the monthly meeting of the Blue Ridge Poets and Authors Guild at the Blue Ridge Mountain Arts Association. It was touching how my fellow authors responded to Doug being there. After the meeting, we took a tour of the art work at the Art Center which is really in a class by itself with local craftsmen and artisans' pieces on display. I was reminded of the time that I dragged Doug and my son Travis to the High Museum in Atlanta to see an exhibit of Freda Kahlo, Diego Rivera, and Picasso. Doug even bought me an art book! I guess it is accurate to say that I meant for them to get some culture. I think that secretly they enjoyed it. Doug certainly seemed to enjoy the gallery in Blue Ridge.

AUGUST 24

We had a laid back morning. Then we headed to Tate, Georgia to visit Gibbs Gardens. The drive there is around forty-five minutes. Since Doug was easily fatigued, we used the shuttle service at the gardens instead of walking the entire time. One section has the largest Japanese Garden in the United States. At the Manor House, Doug made instant friends with the cat. The weather was bright and sunny and not too hot. Doug, being the nursery man that he was, knew a lot of the flowers and plants.

AUGUST 25

We took a drive out Aska Road but spent most of the day just hanging out at the cabin. I had noticed if we were real active one day, it was best to have a restful day afterwards. So, rummy on the deck and more conversation.

"Why did you go into the Marines?"

"Well, Jud and I talked about going into the Army but since Dad was a General and all that we decided not to tell anyone that our Dad was a General and hoped that the Marines would not find out. They found out anyhow. Jud went in first since he graduated first. When I got ready to go in, he told me to be sure NOT to go to Paris Island. He said to tell them I needed to go to the West Coast. They sent me to Paris Island!"

"How was that?"

"Hard."

"I remember when you and Jud were in boot camp you guys started writ-

ing Shelley and me. I was flabbergasted. I don't think either of you had ever written to us before."

"Do you remember me writing you to make sure that there was no perfume or girly stuff on your letters back?"

"Yeah. Why was that?"

"When they had mail call, the Sergeant would sniff the letters and if they smelled girly, he would make a big deal about it. Sometimes we would have to do pushups if we got girly smelling mail. Lucky for me, that never happened. I did get in trouble a lot for being a smartass punk kid."

"What happened?"

"My Sergeant would send me to the Garden."

"What in the world was the Garden?"

"I was given a shovel and told to dig holes. Sometimes I dug for hours. I got in trouble so much they nicknamed me "Digger Doug.""

"That is hilarious! My brother Digger Doug!"

"Alright, Kathywathy."

"Dougiewuggie."

"Martha Gasoline!"

"That's me!"

"I also got in trouble one time when I refused to salute. I had come back from a recon and the guy told me to give him a salute. I said, "You're not an officer so why should I give you a salute!?" He then said, "Smartass, SALUTE means S for size of the unit you reconned, A for the activity they are engaged in, L for the location, U for the kind of unit, T for the time you encountered the unit and E for the equipment the unit has. Now give me the SALUTE!"

"HA! Digger Doug!"

"That's me!"

AUGUST 26

We had big plans for today. We were going to watch my grandson Travis play football. The drive there was around two and a half hours. We would get to see Loralei, Little Ross, and Big Ross as well. Doug was animated and talked a lot as we drove there.

"In Maine I ran cross country. Our school was too small for a football team."

"Were you the fastest one on the team? I think you are still the fastest one in our family as far as running goes."

"No, there was one guy who could beat me. One day I was out running trails and came around a bend and there was this bull moose standing in the path. Scared the crap out of me. I turned around and hauled butt back. I never looked to see if he was going to charge me. I bet I would have outrun that guy that day!"

"When did you run your first marathon?"

"Well, me and this other Marine while we were in Spain got this idea to run the Madrid Marathon. Trouble is we did not really train for it. But we did it anyway. Pretty stupid, but we did stuff like that all the time."

We got to the football game and it was hot but we really enjoyed watching. I cannot remember if they won or lost but as far as our day went, it was a winner. When we got home, we watched the Bucs play the Cleveland Browns. Yeah to football!

AUGUST 27

Today we went to The Blue Ridge Community Theater to watch *One Slight Hitch*. I volunteer there and Doug was able to meet my theater friends. It was a silly comedy, perfect for us. Poor Doug, at age 61 still being dragged around by his big sister to culture stuff!!

AUGUST 28

I got out my fall decorations and Doug supervised. I went ahead and included the Halloween stuff and we had a lot of fun with that. I always like to play with Halloween toys in the stores. I am like a kid and Doug did not like to admit it, but he was just as bad as I was.

AUGUST 29

Today we stayed at the cabin. I worked on some of the wooden furniture on the deck and we played rummy.

"Do you have any regrets?"

"I wish I had stayed in the Marines."

"Why did you leave?"

"I guess because Jud did. We had served two tours. I am not really sure why. But I am glad that I went into the Army Reserves after I got out."

"Why the Army Reserves?"

"Well, at first where we had to go was closer to where I lived. But then everything got moved to Jacksonville. I really liked the military."

"How about the nursery?"

"That was pretty good. I do like working with plants."

"What were some memorable places you went to while you were in the Marines?"

"Well, I got to climb Mount Fuji and the red light district in Amsterdam was really something. One of the weirdest things I saw was people who were cutting the grass in Saudi with little scissors. Also we called the women there, Ninja Women because they were all dressed in black from their heads to their toes. You could hardly even see their eyes."

AUGUST 29

Since we had been out and about the day before, we just chilled out at the cabin. I did some work on the deck with the bar that needed to be sanded and have the polyurethane redone. Doug just watched and told me it looked great. It looked ok, but not great. Some of my sanding looked very amateurish, which is what I was. We watched *Dateline* since we both enjoyed a good murder story every now and then.

I did try again to see if he wanted to do any reading. He and I had often exchanged books and at the cabin I had several that I thought he might like. He loved a good Western and the military genre. But he just was not interested in reading. I think that he did not understand his lack of interest any more than I did.

AUGUST 30

This was another time he came with me to an event I never thought he would have the slightest interest in. My Book Club. Seeing as how he no longer read books, it was somewhat weird. But anyhow, he came along and seemed to be amused by some of the comments. At least he kept a straight face and I had to refrain from looking at him or I would have sniggered or something to that effect. That would not have set well with some of the Book Club attendees. We later laughed about it. It was a good day.

After the Book Club, we took in the sights of downtown Blue Ridge. We visited a few stores, including my favorite one, Multitudes. Multitudes has artist consignments. I have bought a few pieces from there and I always look forward to seeing what is new. My friend, Sue, who was one of my cabin checkers, was working that day and I was glad that she got to see Doug. Before Doug got sick, he met her when we went on a group hike. Doug really liked the artistic trout artwork that was featured all over town.

August 31 was a very eventful day. We gathered our courage and went to the Expedition Bigfoot Museum which is only about a mile from my cabin. There are a lot of people in the mountains who swear that this creature exists, so we wanted to do our due diligence and see what this was all about. We had a ball! We followed that up with *The Hobbit* movie and then the Bucs versus the Redskins to top off the day. We were not thinking very much about pancreatic cancer.

September 1 was a rainy day. Some of my neighbors, two of whom had met Doug on previous visits when we went to Trivia at Fightingtown Tavern, came by to see him. One of them was the retired Marine who had told me about the contaminated wells at Camp LeJeune. Doug was somewhat subdued this day. I do not know if it was the weather or having people visit. Previously, other friends had stopped by and he seemed uncomfortable with all of the attention. He was not extroverted at all. Doug did not like to be the center of attention. I was touched that they came, even though I realized Doug's discomfort. We later watched the Falcons as we talked trash about our respective teams.

September 2. We decided to drive the River Road. It starts in Ducktown and follows the Ocoee River past the Whitewater Center until you reach the outskirts of Cleveland, Tennessee. This was the route we always took when Doug would fly to Chattanooga and I would pick him up. The scenery is always stunning and there are times when I just like to go and drive it. It is one of the places that I take people who come to visit. It goes past the Whitewater Center where the kayaking for the 1996 Atlanta Olympic was held. It is still used today and when the water is up, it is very entertaining to watch the rafts full of people navigating the rapids. In 2015, Shelley, Doug, and I had a vacation at my cabin and one of the activities that we did was white water rafting. I drove through the parking lot at the Center and we watched some rafting for a while before continuing on the drive.

September 3 was drive back to Tampa day. We had a small glitch as we were preparing to leave. Since Doug had been on so many opioids, sometimes he became constipated. At times the bowel movement was so dry that it stopped up the toilet. So of course we had to deal with the toilet. Such fun. Poor Doug.

September 4 was Labor Day and all of Florida was anxiously watching Hurricane Irma. This was especially worrisome for us since Doug's feeding pump needed electricity. We got out our manual and refreshed ourselves on how long the battery would last. It was supposed to work for 24 hours. Ron had a generator at the house where he and Shelley lived so if we were without power for any extended period of time we would have that to help out. We stocked up on some canned goods for those of us that ate. Doug's formula did not have to be refrigerated so that was a plus. Our hospice nurse, Zahra, came by and covered emergency guidelines with us. We felt prepared.

We then went over to Doug's place and Ron took down the window awnings that would be apt to catch the wind and blow away. We secured all the outside of any items that posed the possibility of becoming projectiles.

September 9 Tampa shut down in advance of the storm. Irma arrived on Sunday the 10th. We watched football and listened to the wind and rain. We lost power for around 15 minutes at 9 p.m., but it came back on. We were lucky. Irma, for the Tampa area, proved to be a huge wind event.

The next morning we had no internet or cable. The property was littered with tree limbs. A huge tree that was on a neighbor's side had fallen over onto the fence surrounding the property. Gunn highway was not passable, and many roads were closed. Later in the day, enough of the trees had been removed enough for us to go check Doug's place. It looked fine but had no power. We played cards and picked up limbs and tree debris.

Later in the week, we went to the Lowery Park Zoo. We enjoyed some Stephen King terror by going to see *IT*. Football was now in full swing and I would record the Bucs games in case Doug fell asleep before the game was over.

September 22 I went back to the cabin to support my daughter Liberty as she raced in the Georgia Jewell, a 35-mile endurance trail race. My son Travis was also competing in a bike ride in the mountains called 6 Gap the following day, so I was able to see all of my kids. Lorelei was at Travis' event. I called Doug daily. I headed back to Tampa on the 27th.

Doug was doing pretty well. We were in a comfortable routine of cards, drives, movies, and visits from friends. Every morning we watched The Colbert Report. That always started a conversation.

One of the more distasteful things that we had to do was to get Doug's affairs in order. We had already some experience with that when our parents had died. That did not make it any easier. Who gets what. I could have cared less. Shelley and I were the recipients. The crap you have to do.

October 12 I traveled back to my cabin. Some friends came up and visited for two days and I sold my book at some local festivals before returning to Tampa on the 24th.

It seemed to me that Doug was not doing as well as he had before I left. Perhaps not seeing him every day made me more aware of his health? I am not sure. We always logged how he was doing and he was having more nausea than before. We had known that sooner or later, once he had stopped the chemo that things would take a turn for the worse. On October 31, he stayed in bed almost all day. That was very unusual.

He began to throw up after the refeeds. His pain levels were increasing and on November 7, his fentanyl patches were upped to 75 from 50. The morphine was also increased. He was staying in bed almost every day. He would still shower every night before we hooked him up to the feeding machine and shaved every morning. Shelley moved into the other bedroom in the house with us.

November 8 He requested that we stop the refeeds. We did.

November 9 Doug woke up in the middle of the night with vomiting and nausea. We had even administered more anti nausea drugs from hospice. It was clear that his body could no longer tolerate nutrition. Nutrition had become a source of suffering. He decided to stop all nutrition.

So here we are. Nearing the end of my brother's life. So what do you do? Do you let him see how his suffering is tearing the guts out of you? Do you let him see your pain? Knowing that this will increase his suffering? Or are you seeming to be cold and uncaring if you hide your feelings? How about your sister who wears her heart on her sleeve. More than once she had burst into tears saying, "I guess I am the crybaby of the family."

I would always say, "Well, we need a crybaby in the family, so that is fine." Such a shitty time.

Well, I decided that now was the time to get out the flash drive that I had loaded photos on from several of our trips. The TV was a smart TV and I showed them as a slide. Doug seemed to enjoy this trip back to good memories.

THE TRIP TO SOUTH AMERICA

"Do you remember that first night in Lima? We were all in the same hotel room. The night when we got in very late and you got up at 3 a.m., took a shower and shaved? You had also been snoring. You woke Shelley up and she was roaring mad!"

"Yeah, ha, ha. The two of you got into a fight. She said that you always took my side."

"All I said at first was that you could not control your snoring. She was so mad she said that yes you could, and I argued against that. Then I think I asked her how she could hear you snore when she was deaf in one ear and slept on that good ear. She really went ballistic then."

"Yeah, that was funny later, but not in that moment."

"Yes, we had to leave at 5 in morning and we were tired."

"She is a good sister, even when we push her buttons."

"We all got over it and had a good time."

"We had a fantastic time!"

"Remember this key to our room in the Monastery in The Sacred Valley?"

"Ha ha yes! We almost had to call the hotel guy to work it for us. Especially after we had some Pisco Sours and you had your wine!"

"Macchu Piccu was really something. Those Incas really knew a lot."

"That is you in the lead going to the Sun Gate. We were not allowed to bring water bottles and we were getting pretty thirsty. You kept on going, so Shelley and I sucked it up and went on."

"Ha ha look at Shelley threatening to push me off!"

"The Galapagos were pretty awesome as well."

"Yeah, you could make a lot of turtle soup with those tortoises. Also I did not know that boobies had blue feet."

"Doug Miller!"

"Ha ha. Just kidding, Kathywathy."

"Hey remember this one? This is from your birthday week when Shelley gave you a plane ticket up to my place in 2015. We went and hiked at Amicalola Falls."

"That was a lot of fun."

"Brasstown Bald was pretty cool too!"

"Ha, ha! What was the name of this bar that you dragged me to?"
"This was at Blue Ridge Brewery."

"Watch out there is a shark behind you!"
"That is a really great aquarium you guys have. It is better than the one we have in Tampa."

"Do you remember this place?"

"Raven Cliff Falls, right?"

"Correct. There were even some yellow jackets close to where we had our lunch, not good for me and my allergy to them. But we got out unscathed. That is Mike Pilvinsky behind you."

"Yeah. I really enjoyed talking to him about the military."

"I remember this place. You took me to Helen and we ate at that German place. We ate wiener schnitzel. Really good food and the drive there was really nice."

"Now we are looking at our sibling vacation in 2016."
"You wore me and Shelley out. We had to go home and rest for a week!"

"Oh this was the day we rented a canoe and canoed on Lake Blue Ridge! That marina had a lot of cool stuff in it."

"Here we are at the Carter Presidential Library. We started there and then went to the Atlanta Botanical Gardens where there was a Chilhuli Exhibit."

"I remember Dad taking us to the one in Tacoma. It was really something."

"I think I liked this one best of all."

"You look like you almost like her. Ha just kidding."
"Yeah, I guess we need to keep her."

"I remember this. You tried to get us killed. And you almost took Shelley out with your foot when you came in too fast on the zip line!"

"It wasn't my fault. That guide was pushing me off the platform before Shelley was out of the way on the next platform. I did get her right in the mouth. That was not good. But we survived."

"Oh, this was that Hillbilly music place."

"It's called Pickin in the Park. I thought you would get into it since you like country music."

"That was not country music and some of those people must have problems with their hearing 'cause their singing was awful."

"Bruhahaha!"

"This was a hike at Carters Lake, The Amadahy Trail. Liberty had come and was with us. Why are you hiding?"

"I don't like to have my picture taken."

"Well, we took it anyway."

"That hike was what we call "Hike and Wine." The winery was fun."
"That was with those women you hang out with. What are they called?"
"The Blue Jays."

"Here we are at the Ocoee Whitewater Center."
"It was pretty funny to watch some of the rafts capsize!"

"This was at Fall Branch Falls."
"Like I said, you wore us out!"

"Well, at least you would sleep well!"

"Oh this was the trip to Vegas! That ride in the desert was really great."

"Hey this is the day we rode that Santa Train in Blue Ridge. Remember when the Grinch was on the train and Little Ross begged him not to steal his Christmas toys?"

"Yeah that was pretty funny. There you are hiding in the back again."

"I told you. I don't like to have my picture taken."

"Well, we took it anyway. Again Douglas. HA!"

"Kathywathy."

"Little Travis' football game! We got to see them every time I came to visit you! It was hilarious watching them sometimes."

"This was on the way to Jekyll Island."
"Looks creepy especially after that movie came out."

"Crap, I remember this game you took me to. The Bucs led all the way until the 4th quarter."

"It was fun anyhow."

"It was more fun when they were winning!"

"Ha!"

"Cumberland Island where those wild horses are. I really liked this. Didn't we also go deep sea fishing? You took me as your guest to your store convention."

"Yes, we had a good time."

"This was also in Jacksonville. I used to come to visit you in Waycross for New Years and we always ran that race that was before a parade. They had a really good parade, the Clydesdales and a lot of those Star Wars fanatics dressed in costume."

"I really liked the route of the race. All along the St John's River."

"This was one of the last trips to Dad's. What was the name of this restaurant?"

"I think it was the Red Robin or something. Dad really loved to take us to burger places when we came out. I don't think June cared for them too much. I remember one visit Travis and I went out there and guess where he took us for lunch right after we landed? Jack in the Box, and this was the year when a bunch of people had died from eating their burgers! Dad said it was really safe since a bunch of people had gotten sick so they were really trying to be safe. I got a chicken sandwich but Travis and Dad got burgers… medium rare even!"

"I really miss Dad and Mom. Jud too."

"Yeah."

November 11 I was scheduled to sell my book at the Saturday Market at the local mall and Doug wanted to come and see it. Here is my brother, no longer getting any nutrition and yet he wants to visit me and the book. He liked the book. I used to joke with him that he liked it because I told the world about how I allowed my baby brother to take the rap for me when I drank our Dad's coca cola. Doug said he just was in a hurry to go and play and Dad didn't really spank very hard. So he admitted to a crime he did not commit while I was the guilty one who remained silent until I wrote the book.

We had let all of the kids know that he was declining and was no longer receiving any nutrition. On November 12, Lorelei and Little Travis came to see him. Marissa also came. We watched the Bucs and I began to put on soothing music from the TV when he would drift off.

Ninja was sleeping regularly with Doug.

November 14 Loralei and Little Travis leave and Liberty and Big Travis arrived. Doug's pain meds had been increased and he was often hallucinating. November 15, Ryan flew in from Tennessee. Doug was staying in bed almost all day now. But we did watch the Bucs. He seemed to be enjoying some of his hallucinations. He told Liberty that there were people coming out of the ceiling and that there were clouds everywhere. Often when asked how he was doing he would say, "Oh, I'm just floating. It's nice and floaty here."

We talked about the Chinese and cranes. Cranes were supposed to appear and take you to heaven or the great beyond. And we had our regular Sand Hill cranes that we could see just outside Doug's window.

November 19 The kids had to leave. We watched the Bucs play but he slept most of the day.

Liberty came back on the 21st. Thanksgiving was on the 23rd. Liberty, Marissa, and I went and did the Turkey Trot in St Petersburg. That afternoon we took shifts going to Shelley and Ron's for Thanksgiving. It was such a hollow holiday. Travis and Ashli came down.

By now he was too weak to walk. The hospice nurses were coming and bathing him. We had gotten a portable potty chair. He was still getting some water as we had to flush his tube to get medications into his system. Knowing that the water flush was prolonging his life, but necessary to keep him from suffering pain, was making me crazy.

I had found a soft music station on TV that had beautiful scenery to watch along with the soothing melodies. It was like you have in the background at a spa. He seemed to like it. He was becoming comatose but peaceful. No more nausea, diarrhea, or vomiting, but now he is fading away.

November 27 Shelley had gone bowling and would be home around 10 p.m. I was watching some TV and looking in on Doug from time to time. Around 7 p.m. he started to get out of bed, which he had tried to do a few times before. He said he had to get out of there.

I said, "Dougie what can I do for you? You can't get out of bed you are too weak right now."

He said, "Somebody just shoot me! I am not dying!"

So I am crying and trying to keep him from falling and I heard myself weep the words, "Yes Doug, you are."

When my Dad was sick and close to the end of his life I had been with him when he said,"I can't sleep. I just want to die." He would pace and then collapse into his chair.

Now to hear this from Doug was so overwhelming, so awful, awful.

He was so very agitated and I knew that he was too weak to walk anywhere and I was terrified that I would be unable to keep him from falling and injuring himself. He tried to fight me as I tried to persuade him to stay in the bed. I was hugging him and also struggling to get him to stay in the bed. I called hospice and they instructed me to give him some medication for anxiety that we had on hand. They said they could have a nurse there soon. I also called Shelley in a panic. I was finally able to get the medication into him and he began to settle down. By the time Shelley and the nurse arrived he was stabilized.

November 28 There is a terrible beauty in his dying. Exquisite and elegant. Yet he has become a corpse that breathes. Every four hours he is given 20 ml of morphine and lorazepam. Does he hear us? Where is he? Where has he gone? When I awake in the night I can hear him breathe. I go in and kiss his forehead. His breathing is loud and deep, but not labored. Almost like the deepest of sighs. A serenity has enveloped him.

And we wait.

November 30 He is now incontinent, something that he was not until he became comatose. Hospice came and put a catheter in to better manage his incontinence. He became quite agitated when this happened. It would turn out to be the last time we saw any sign of him being in the present. He went back to his serenity.

December 5 We had discovered that the area around the catheter was going to have to be cleaned daily. Doug had discussed early on that he did not want Shelley or I doing anything that would involve his private parts and that if it came to that, he wanted to go into a nursing facility.

So around 10 that morning we called hospice to discuss a nursing facility. They said they would send someone out.

After the call, Shelley went into his room to look in on him. She came out and said, "I think he is gone."

December 5 was our Dad's birthday.

We like to think that he did not want to miss the birthday party. Ron said that he heard us discussing the nursing facility and decided it was "time to get the heck out of here."

And now we weep. Empty and hollow, we fall into the abyss.

Semper Fi, Doug. Do or die.

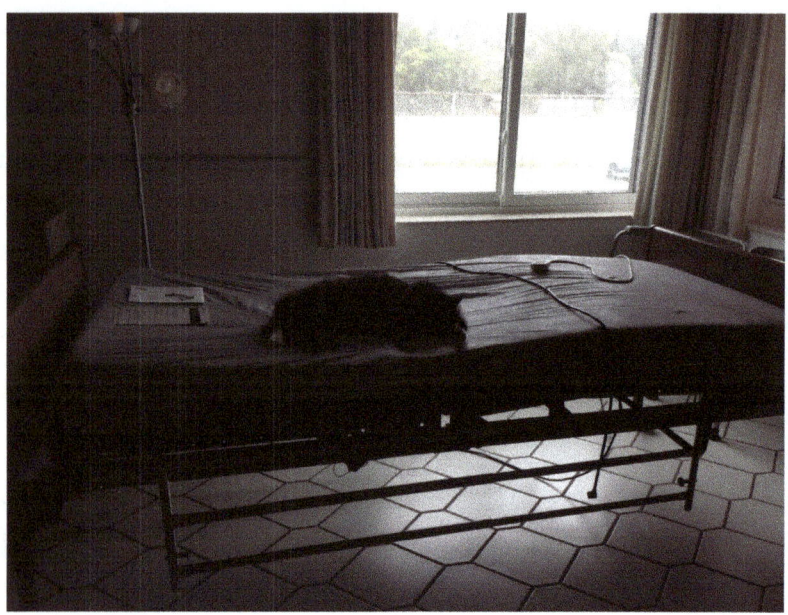

Afterword

Doug was cremated. On February 23, 2018, we gathered the family together for a small Celebration of Life service that Shelley had asked Doug if it would be alright with him to do. It was touching, tearful, and yet there was a sad joy in that time. His ashes were put in the National Cemetery right next to our mother. This had also been his wish. The Marines did him proud as his flag was given to us and taps was played. The following day we ran in the Gasparilla Races like we had done so many times before. I felt like Doug was there in the race somewhere.

Shelley wanted me to have Doug's flag. When we were going through his things, we found that he had saved his high school cross country shoes. It made us cry all over again. So I decide that I had to keep them. Now they are part of his flag and stay in what was his room at my cabin. I keep his photo on my dresser and I like to touch him on the forehead every now and then. Digger Doug.

12-24-17

dear Kathy + family,
    I am so sorry to hear abo Doug's passing earlier this month. He was such a special patient to me and I am forever grateful I was able to be a part of your family's stay. Do you know how many people I've said "you look good today!" to? Probably thousands of patients -- and he is the only one to have said back to me "Thanks! You do too!" with a smile. His upbeat attitude & strength are admirable. The way you + your sister cared for him is remarkable and is the reason he did as well as he did. ⟶

You have an amazing family. Wishing you all a better 2018 but doug will certainly never be forgotten.

Fondly,
Samantha Sheng

www.ingramcontent.com/pod-product-compliance
Ingram Content Group UK Ltd.
Pitfield, Milton Keynes, MK11 3LW, UK
UKHW021256180426
11947UKWH00011B/812